HAMZA AYUB & ALISHQUICHE

THE CONTENT CREATOR'S COMPASS

A BATTLE-TESTED GUIDE
TO SUCCEEDING ONLINE AS
AN INFLUENCER AND BRAND

Published by
LID Publishing
An imprint of LID Business Media Ltd.
LABS House, 15-19 Bloomsbury Way,
London, WC1A 2TH, UK

info@lidpublishing.com
www.lidpublishing.com

A member of:

BPR
businesspublishersroundtable.com

All rights reserved. Without limiting the rights under copyright reserved, no part of this publication may be reproduced, stored or introduced into a retrieval system, or transmitted, in any form or by any means (electronic, mechanical, photocopying, recording or otherwise) without the prior written permission of both the copyright owners and the publisher of this book.

© Hamza Ayub & Alishquiche, 2025
© LID Business Media Limited, 2025

Printed by Short Run Press Limited
ISBN: 978-1-917391-16-0
ISBN: 978-1-917391-17-7 (ebook)

Cover and page design: Caroline Li

HAMZA AYUB & ALISHQUICHE

THE CONTENT CREATOR'S COMPASS

A BATTLE-TESTED GUIDE
TO SUCCEEDING ONLINE AS
AN INFLUENCER AND BRAND

MADRID | MEXICO CITY | LONDON
BUENOS AIRES | BOGOTA | SHANGHAI

CONTENTS

HOW TO READ YOUR COMPASS
— Introduction — 1

CHAPTER 1
The Ten Commandments of Successful
Content Creation — 6

CHAPTER 2
The 12 Categories of Content Creation — 16

CHAPTER 3
Finding Your Niche and Understanding
the Content Landscape — 36

CHAPTER 4
The Ten How-Tos in Content Creation — 58

CHAPTER 5
Crafting Superior Value for Your Audience — 66

CHAPTER 6
Navigating Your Positioning 82

CHAPTER 7
Follower Dissonance 90

CHAPTER 8
Key Lessons in Entrepreneurial Thinking 100

CHAPTER 9
Push vs Pull: Strategically Reaching Your Audience . . . 110

CHAPTER 10
Crafting Effective Advertisements – Brand Deals 122

CHAPTER 11
Navigating the Art of Native Advertising 148

CHAPTER 12
Creative Block 154

CHAPTER 13
The Six-Step Approach to Cultivating Fans 164

CHAPTER 14
Mastering Social Media: Navigating Advantages
and Challenges 172

LET'S GO!
Your Content Creation Journey Awaits 181

AUTHORS' BIOGRAPHY 184

HOW TO READ YOUR COMPASS
– INTRODUCTION

The world of online content is here to stay, and that's something we need to fully acknowledge. The virtual and offline spaces have merged, making adaptation not just necessary but inevitable. Full-blown careers are built on content creation, businesses employing hundreds have emerged, and those who understand its importance – be it companies or individuals – are thriving. Despite this, the field of content creation still lacks the clear categorization and guidance that established professions enjoy.

This book seeks to fill that gap.

Whether you're just starting out, refining your craft or building from scratch, the insights in this book will be your compass. It will guide you in crafting your personal brand and in driving the long-term growth of your business.

Learn how to read and navigate the social online world authentically, transparently and engagingly. Each chapter concludes with an exercise to help you reflect and design your personal strategy or refine your content creation and marketing efforts.

Typically, corporate marketing strategies and influencer advice are tackled separately. However, drawing from our personal and professional experiences over the past years, the authors of this book believe in the synergy between these perspectives. Understanding both the corporate and influencer sides of content creation is crucial. So, whether you're a corporate marketer, an aspiring influencer or a business owner, this book is for you.

To make this book more enjoyable, the two authors decided not to differentiate who is speaking but rather stick to 'we' and draw from both our experiences and knowledge.

Try to view each chapter from both the corporate and influencer perspectives to maximize your benefits.

THE CONTENT CREATOR'S COMPASS AND YOU

Content creation often feels confined to the virtual world and isolated from the physical, but this doesn't make it any less real. Every action in the virtual space leads to tangible impacts. Whether your goal is sales, exposure, brand awareness or entertainment, approaches may differ, but the core principles remain the same. The nuances are in the execution.

We've structured this book as a step-by-step guide. Every chapter includes an exercise for you to work on, and whenever we've thought it helpful, we have included our own examples from corporate and influencer activity, or illustrated them based on three imaginary creators:
- Jeff The Car Company, a company selling electric cars.
- Harley326, an influencer specializing in dance challenges.
- Jason Big Muscles, a workout professional. Quick, effective workouts for busy people.

This book is a journey, and we start it with the 'Ten Commandments' of successful content creation, which will serve as your roadmap. We'll also show you how to stay consistent with your format and strategy, by introducing influencer categories. You will then dive into defining your potential niche(s) and explore how you can understand the environment you operate within (Content Landscape). Once you've gained a good understanding and oriented yourself, we'll address the most common 'How to do Content Creation' questions. You will then be ready to focus on defining the value your content should provide (Crafting Value for Your Audience to Create Superior Value).

Next, we'll look into positioning – helping your audience find and connect with you amid today's information overload. Positioning is crucial, but it's just the start. You will gain insights in how to avoid follower dissonance and stay true to your brand and message (checklists included).

You'll then be ready for an outlook on advanced strategies, covering the journey from cultivating an entrepreneurial mindset to maintaining audience engagement, mastering authentic advertising and leveraging native ads. And when you're hit with the inevitable creative block, we will provide you with strategies to help you overcome it.

CHAPTER 1

THE TEN COMMANDMENTS OF SUCCESSFUL CONTENT CREATION

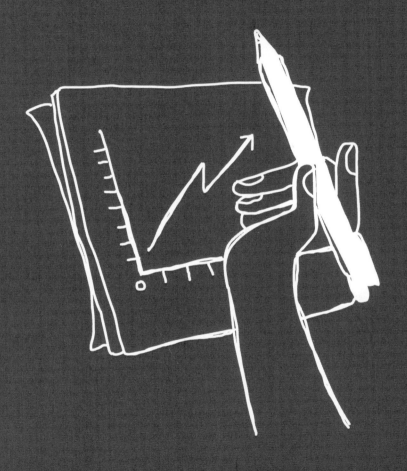

This chapter is what sparked the idea for this entire book during a creative online brainstorming session between the two authors, when Alishquiche was just starting out with 50,000 followers. Hamza scribbled down these ten commandments and sent them to Alishquiche, and the next thing you know, we kept this going. We wrote a note here and there, and eventually, we put them together and refined them. Two years and many international keynote speeches later, we thought to ourselves, why not write a book? Lo and behold, here it is.

As the title suggests, this book can't hold all the answers; content creation is a journey shaped according to your own needs. However, what we reveal in this book has successfully led many creators and celebrities in our circle to the promised land, and perhaps it can get you there too.

These ten guiding rules – or 'commandments' – are timeless pillars that will help you produce consistently high-quality content, engage your audience and build a brand that thrives in a competitive space.

CHAPTER 1
THE TEN COMMANDMENTS OF SUCCESSFUL CONTENT CREATION

1. **THOU SHALT KNOW THY AUDIENCE**

   Understanding your audience is the foundation of all successful content creation. Without a clear grasp of who you're speaking to, your content will lack focus and relevance.

   Example: Emma Chamberlain built her YouTube career by connecting deeply with her young audience. Her content revolves around the everyday experiences of Gen Z, such as navigating school, friendships and self-discovery. Her authenticity and openness about her struggles make her relatable and convey the feeling of listening to a friend. By knowing what her audience relates to, she continues to create videos that resonate, which has helped her build a loyal fanbase.

2. **THOU SHALT PROVIDE VALUE ABOVE ALL ELSE**

   Content without value is just noise. Whether your goal is to entertain, inform or inspire, every piece of content you create should deliver value.

   Example: Nas Daily is known for his one-minute daily videos on Facebook, TikTok and Instagram. He travels around the world, creating educational and inspiring content, often highlighting underrepresented stories and global perspectives. Each video delivers clear value in the form of insight or inspiration from around the world, which keeps his audience coming back every day.

3. THOU SHALT BE CONSISTENT

Consistency is the key to building a lasting relationship with your audience. Whether it's posting weekly videos or daily updates, set a schedule and stick to it.

Example: Charli D'Amelio, one of TikTok's biggest stars, gained massive popularity by consistently posting dance videos and collaborating with other creators. Her regular posting helped her amass a huge following and maintain her audience's interest in the fast-paced world of TikTok.

4. THOU SHALT ADAPT AND EVOLVE

While consistency is crucial, so is the ability to adapt. The digital world rapidly evolves, and content that worked a year ago may not resonate today.

Example: PewDiePie started his career as a gaming YouTuber, but his content has evolved into exploring commentary, reaction videos and social issues. His willingness to adapt while staying true to his core personality meant he was one of YouTube's most popular creators for over a decade.

5. THOU SHALT BE AUTHENTIC

In a world of polished personas, authenticity is your greatest asset. Followers connect with creators who are real, relatable and transparent, and who are also passionate about their content. You should create the kind of content you enjoy repeatedly making.

Example: Liza Koshy's rise to fame came from her funny, raw and unfiltered personality. Whether on Vine, YouTube or TikTok, Liza's goofy and relatable humour feels genuine and has endeared her to millions of fans. She isn't afraid to laugh at herself, and that authenticity keeps her audience engaged.

6. THOU SHALT ENGAGE WITH THY COMMUNITY

Engaging with your audience is just as important as creating content for them. Respond to comments, ask questions, hold polls and encourage feedback.

Example: Known for his large-scale challenges and philanthropy, MrBeast actively engages with his community through social media comments, giveaways and participatory challenges. He often includes his followers in his videos and bases some content ideas on audience suggestions, which has helped to build his strong social media community. However, he is also a good example of what happens if followers discover discrepancies between the content communicated and life lived (Google search: MrBeast controversy). Followers assume your online personality reflects your authentic self, and as soon as there is a perceived discrepancy, they will communicate that.

7. THOU SHALT MEASURE AND OPTIMIZE

You need to know what's working and what isn't. Use analytics to track performance indicators like engagement, watch time and conversions, and tweak your content strategy accordingly.

Example: Gary Vaynerchuk (GaryVee) is a social media entrepreneur, who actively tracks performance across platforms. He regularly adjusts his content strategy based on what resonates most with his audience. Whether it's his short motivational clips or long-form business advice, Gary uses data to refine his content and maximize its impact.

8. THOU SHALT EXPERIMENT FEARLESSLY

Successful creators aren't afraid to try new things. The digital landscape is ever-changing, and so are the tastes of your audience. Experimentation allows you to discover new opportunities.

Example: Marques Brownlee (MKBHD) is known for his tech reviews. He experiments with new content formats like interviews with CEOs, long-form podcasts and testing products in unique ways. His willingness to innovate has helped him stay at the top of the tech content space for years.

9. THOU SHALT FOCUS ON QUALITY OVER QUANTITY

While it's important to be consistent, quality trumps quantity. It's better to produce fewer pieces of high-quality, engaging content than to churn out content lacking depth or purpose.

Example: Jenn Im, a YouTube fashion and lifestyle creator, is known for her beautifully curated, high-quality videos. She focuses on producing polished and well-thought-out content, rather than posting constantly. This attention to detail helps her maintain a premium brand image and a loyal audience.

10. THOU SHALT STAY TRUE TO THY VISION

It's easy to get swept up in trends or pressures to conform, but staying true to your vision is key to lasting success. Your unique voice and perspective are what will set you apart.

Example: Casey Neistat's signature style of vlogging – fast cuts, cinematic shots, and meaningful storytelling – redefined the YouTube landscape. Even as new trends emerged, Casey remained true to his vision of creating story-driven content. His authenticity and refusal to follow trends have made him one of the most respected creators on YouTube.

The path to becoming a successful content creator is paved with challenges, but by following these **Ten Commandments**, you can build a brand that thrives. From knowing your audience and providing value, to staying consistent and true to your vision, these guiding principles are designed to help you create content that resonates, engages and ultimately drives long-term success.

Remember, successful content creation isn't about quick wins or viral moments – it's about building a legacy through meaningful, authentic and valuable content that deeply connects with your audience.

CHAPTER 2

THE 12 CATEGORIES OF CONTENT CREATION

In every field, categorization is essential for understanding the available options and determining your specialisms. Just as doctors in medicine choose specialities like cardiology or surgery, content creators also operate within distinct categories. However, unlike established professions, the world of content creation has lacked clear categorization and guidance. This has left many individual and corporate content creators navigating blindly, making it difficult to maintain consistency and direction.

We often see people attending keynotes, events or online courses about becoming a better content creator, only to find these programs rarely mention a crucial truth: *becoming a successful online creator often involves selecting one of many established fields – a role that can easily demand 100% of your time and energy.*

To help you get started, we've compiled a table of **12 distinct content creation categories**, with examples. While these categories might not fully resonate with you, you may recognize some of the influencers listed in the example column (we encourage you to explore their channels and content online). Our list is not exhaustive and will evolve over time.

The concept of **creator categories** provides a structured framework for content creation, enabling individuals and organizations to effectively channel their efforts. By selecting a category that aligns with your passions and strengths, you can streamline your content creation process, build expertise and significantly improve your chances of success.

CHAPTER 2
THE 12 CATEGORIES OF CONTENT CREATION

At the end of this book, you may come back to this chapter's exercise and reevaluate in which category you think you belong.

THE 12 CONTENT CREATION CATEGORIES

CATEGORY	CHARACTERISTICS	EXAMPLES
REACTORS	real-time, authentic reactions, often using humour, sarcasm or critique to connect with viewers	Khaby Lame, Joey Swoll, Paul Olima
TREND PERPETUATORS	typically have a keen sense of what will go viral, producing quick, engaging and highly shareable content	Charli D'Amelio, Kris8an (Kris Grippo), Addison Rae
FLEXERS	high production quality, polished visuals and a confident tone	Dan Bilzerian
PIONEERS	introducing new formats, styles or genres of content, setting standards for others to follow	Casey Neistat, MrBeast, PewDiePie, Emma Chamberlain
ACCIDENTALY FAMOUS	raw, unpolished and unintentional	Hasbulla, Hawk Tuah Girl
FLAGRANTS	raw, unapologetic and deliberately confrontational	Candace Ovens, Dave Rubin, The Majority Report
AGGREGATORS	often analytical, incorporating commentary, visuals or text to break down complex information	What Culture, HasanAbi, Philip DeFranco

THE CONTENT CREATOR'S COMPASS

CATEGORY	CHARACTERISTICS	EXAMPLES
THIRST TRAPS	carefully curated aesthetics and an emphasis on visual allure	Vinnie Hacker, Mowgli
LEGACY MEDIA & TRADITIONALISTS	high-production value of their traditional media background while adapting their content	Keye & Peele, College Humor, Gilly and Keeves, WWE, Piers Morgan Uncensored
STREAMERS	real-time interaction with viewers	Ninja, Vaush
GURUS	authoritative, yet approachable, using step-by-step explanations, demonstrations and motivational messages to inspire	Grant Cordone, Athlean-X, Pamela Reif
ONE-HIT WONDERS	uniqueness or novelty, but the inability to consistently produce equally engaging material leads to a rapid decline in public interest	Backpack Kid, Damn Daniel

CHAPTER 2
THE 12 CATEGORIES OF CONTENT CREATION

If you want to achieve online success, it's crucial to first understand the different creator categories and identify which one best aligns with your interests, skills and goals. Once you grasp these concepts, you'll never see your favourite influencers or online personalities in the same way again – you'll start to recognize them grouped into distinct categories.

To illustrate these categories, we will look at examples of successful creators who have carved out niches within their respective fields. By studying their strategies and approaches, you can gain valuable insights into how to thrive within your chosen category through consistency and by drawing inspiration from them.

As you explore the creator categories in this chapter, reflect on your own strengths, preferences and goals. By completing the exercise and identifying the category that best aligns with your interests and aspirations, you can chart a clear path and set yourself up for success in the dynamic world of content creation.

1. REACTORS

Reactors create content where they respond to or provide commentary on various forms of media, such as viral videos, news clips, music or trends. For industry specialists like doctors, this could involve reacting to user-generated health advice and evaluating it from a professional perspective. From a corporate angle, it might mean reacting to product-related content or sharing expertise – e.g., a travel insurance company could provide advice on user-generated content about lost luggage, offering practical tips on handling the situation.

Reactors' content is characterized by real-time, authentic reactions, often incorporating humour, sarcasm or critique to engage viewers. Their appeal lies in the shared experience, making audiences feel validated or entertained by the creator's perspective on trending topics.

Examples:
> **Khaby Lame:** Famous for his humorous, silent reactions to overly complicated life hacks, delivered with his signature expressions.
> **Joey Swoll:** Provides commentary on gym etiquette and fitness culture, reacting to fitness-related content with a focus on promoting positive gym environments.
> **Paul Olima:** Offers comical reactions to fitness trends and myths.

2. TREND PERPETUATORS

Trend Perpetuators excel at identifying and amplifying social media trends, such as viral challenges, dances or memes. They play a key role in spreading trends by showcasing their version of popular content and encouraging others to join in. These creators have **a knack for spotting what will go viral and producing quick, shareable content** to keep the trend alive.

Examples:
> - **Charli D'Amelio:** One of the most prominent social media stars, known for creating and popularizing viral dance trends replicated worldwide.
> - **Addison Rae:** Another leading figure in popularizing dance routines and trends, often through collaborations.

Important Note: Not everyone who engages with trends falls into this category. Trend perpetuators focus their entire content strategy on reacting to and creating trends, aiming to go viral as frequently as possible.

For example, let's examine two past trends: "Two Types of People" and "Looking for a Man in Finance" (if unfamiliar, a quick web search will provide context). A true trend perpetuator would create multiple videos adapting these concepts to different topics, keeping their content highly shareable.

For creators or companies with specific focuses – like promoting sci-fi books or selling beverages – the approach should be more deliberate. Evaluate trends carefully and adapt them meaningfully to align with your goals.

Examples: Alishquiche seamlessly aligned the "Two Types of People" trend with her niche, creating a video titled "Two Types of People Watching Movies." This content deeply resonated with her followers because it was authentic and perfectly complemented her usual focus on movies and books. Rather than jumping on the bandwagon, Alishquiche tailored the trend to fit her brand identity, thereby reinforcing her unique voice and style while enhancing her connection with her audience.

From a corporate perspective, Dunkin' Switzerland demonstrated a masterclass in trend adaptation with the "Looking for a Man in Finance" trend. Rather than having employees parrot the viral lines – a move that would have offered minimal value to their audience – they cleverly printed the trend's lyrics on their iconic donuts. This approach not only stayed true to Dunkin's brand but also aligned naturally with their followers' interests: donuts and coffee. By leveraging the trend in a way that felt organic and on-brand, Dunkin' Switzerland managed to engage their audience meaningfully while strengthening their brand connection.

3. FLEXERS

Flexers focus on showcasing wealth, success or a luxurious lifestyle. Their content often features high-end items, exotic vacations or impressive fitness achievements. This category is characterized by polished visuals and a confident tone. While some view them as aspirational, others see them as over-the-top, sparking both admiration and controversy.

Example:
- **Dan Bilzerian**: Known for flaunting his lavish lifestyle, featuring luxury cars, private jets and extravagant parties.

4. PIONEERS

Pioneers are trailblazers who introduce new formats, styles or genres of content, setting the standard for others. Their innovative approaches redefine how audiences engage with certain topics, whether through storytelling, groundbreaking editing or entirely new content concepts.

Examples:
- **Casey Neistat**: Revolutionized the daily vlog genre with his cinematic storytelling and unique editing style.
- **MrBeast**: Known for large-scale, often philanthropic challenges, pushing the boundaries of viral content.

> **PewDiePie**: One of the earliest gaming YouTubers who set the benchmark for gaming and commentary content.
> **Emma Chamberlain**: Brought a fresh, relatable style to vlogging with her candid, quirky personality and innovative editing, inspiring a new generation of creators.

5. ACCIDENTALLY FAMOUS

This category refers to individuals who gain fame unexpectedly, often through a single viral moment, meme or unplanned post. Unlike traditional influencers, they did not initially set out to build an online presence. Instead, their fame is a product of the unpredictable nature of social media algorithms and audience engagement.

Their content style is **typically raw, unpolished and unintentional**, which contributes to their charm and authenticity. Audiences are often captivated by their stories because they weren't actively seeking fame. However, maintaining this newfound fame can be challenging, as it heavily depends on how well they adapt to the sudden spotlight. Some may embrace the opportunity, transitioning into a sustained content creation journey, while others may choose to retreat back into anonymity.

Examples:
- **Hasbulla Magomedov**: A regular individual who became a social media sensation after a series of playful, unintentional clips featuring his humorous antics and unique personality went viral, including his mock 'fight' challenges and interactions with MMA stars.
- **Hawk Tuah Girl**: A regular individual who became a social media sensation after a short, unintentional clip in another creator's street interview went viral, featuring her unique "Hawk Tuah" response.

It's important to distinguish the "Accidentally Famous" from **One-Hit Wonders**. While One-Hit Wonders often fade after their burst of popularity, the Accidentally Famous manage to sustain their fame – either through their own efforts or with external support. They capitalize on their viral moment and successfully build on it, maintaining relevance in the public eye. This makes them more than just a fleeting internet sensation; they transition from a single viral incident to ongoing recognition.

From a corporate perspective, partnering with an Accidentally Famous creator can present opportunities for long-term engagement and brand association.

6. FLAGRANTS

Flagrants thrive on controversy, shock value or pushing societal boundaries. Their content often involves provocative opinions, edgy humour or defiant actions that challenge social norms and the status quo. By sparking debates or eliciting strong reactions, they draw significant attention and engagement, though they risk polarizing their audience. Their style is **raw, unapologetic and deliberately confrontational**.

Examples:
> - **Candace Owens**: Known for her provocative political commentary, often sparking intense debate on social media.
> - **Dave Rubin**: Engages in controversial political and social discussions, challenging mainstream viewpoints.
> - **The Majority Report**: A political commentary platform known for its sharp critiques of right-wing ideologies and its confrontational, satirical take on mainstream political narratives.

7. AGGREGATORS

Aggregators focus on curating and summarizing content from various sources. They provide viewers with a comprehensive overview of specific topics, news or trends by collecting information and presenting it in an easily digestible format. Their style is often analytical, incorporating **commentary, visuals or text to break down complex information**, making it accessible to a broader audience.

Examples:
> **WhatCulture**: Curates and presents content related to pop culture, entertainment and media.
> **HasanAbi**: Streams and analyses political events and social issues, providing commentary and summarizing complex topics.
> **Philip DeFranco**: Offers news roundups and pop culture commentary, breaking down current events in a concise and engaging manner.

8. **THIRST TRAPS**

Thirst Traps are creators who post content designed to attract attention through physical appeal. They often use alluring poses, clothing or suggestive captions to generate engagement in the form of likes, comments and shares. While commonly found in fitness and lifestyle niches, this category emphasizes curated aesthetics and visual allure.

Examples:
> **Vinnie Hacker**: Leverages his physical appeal and fashion sense to create stylized, visually captivating content.
> **Mowgli**: Focuses on fashion and lifestyle content, frequently highlighting personal style and physical aesthetics.

9. LEGACY MEDIA & TRADITIONALISTS

Legacy Media & Traditionalists are individuals or brands that originated in traditional media (e.g. TV, newspapers, radio) and have transitioned into the digital space. They maintain the structured, high-production value of their traditional media background while adapting their content for online consumption.

Examples:
- **Piers Morgan Uncensored**: Transitioned from traditional television to digital platforms while retaining a formal, structured interview style.
- **Key & Peele**: Originally a television sketch comedy duo, they have successfully adapted their content for online audiences.
- **College Humor**: Evolved from a website into a digital sketch comedy hub.
- **Gilly and Keeves**: Produces TV-style sketch comedy adapted for digital platforms.
- **WWE**: Once rooted in televised sports entertainment, WWE now actively leverages digital platforms to expand their storytelling through individual stage character accounts.

10. STREAMERS

Streamers broadcast live video content, often involving gaming, live commentary, tutorials or interactive Q&A sessions. They foster a sense of community through **real-time interaction with viewers** via live chat. Streamers must balance spontaneity with entertainment, using a casual, conversational tone to keep their audience engaged.

Examples:
> **Ninja**: A renowned gaming streamer, primarily known for his live Fortnite gameplay and engaging interactions with viewers.
> **Vaush**: Focuses on political debates and discussions, live streaming commentary on current events.

11. GURUS

Gurus specialise in niche areas such as fitness, finance, beauty or self-improvement. They position themselves as experts, offering tips, tutorials, advice and guidance. Their style is authoritative yet approachable, using step-by-step explanations, demonstrations and motivational messages to inspire their audience.

Examples:
> **Grant Cardone**: Focuses on finance, entrepreneurship and personal growth, sharing practical tips and motivational advice.
> **Pamela Reif**: A fitness influencer known for her instructional workout videos and healthy lifestyle content.

12. ONE-HIT WONDERS

One-Hit Wonders are creators who achieve explosive fame due to a single viral piece of content. Despite attempts to sustain their popularity, they often struggle to replicate their initial success. Their content is typically unique or novel, but the inability to consistently produce equally engaging material leads to a rapid decline in public interest.

Examples:
> **Backpack Kid**: Gained fame for the "flossing" dance, which unexpectedly went viral.
> **Damn Daniel**: Known for a viral video featuring the catchphrase "Damn, Daniel!"

Now that you have a clear understanding of the categories and their characteristics, let's engage in an exercise, which provides a structured approach to identifying your category. As an example, we've completed the exercise ourselves. As mentioned, you may come back to this category exercise once you have reached the end of the book and reevaluate your category.

This exercise is about defining what aligns with your strengths and feels authentic to you, while also meeting your audience's expectations. By committing to a specific category, you can streamline your efforts and move forward with a clear sense of direction. Keep in mind that your category is not set in stone. As your approach evolves, your category may shift accordingly. Embrace this flexibility as part of your growth journey.

EXERCISE:
FIND YOUR CATEGORY

Step 1: Answer these questions:

- In what form and style would you like to present your content?

  _____

  _____

- Is there an existing creator you can draw inspiration from, offering similar passion or expertise? (This may require some research.)

  _____

  _____

Step 2: Compare the highlights from Step 1 with the characteristics of the categories in the table on pages 19–20. Identify any overlaps with a category or creators listed in the table, as well as any creator you mentioned in Step 1.

Step 3: Determine the category where you see the most alignment. Ideally, find a creator in this category who can serve as inspiration.

My Category

_____

_____

EXERCISE RESPONSE EXAMPLE: FIND YOUR CATEGORY

In what form and style would you like to present your content?
We want to break down the book's information in a visually appealing, easy-to-digest format. Our content will feature commentary, step-by-step analyses, and examples. We will also answer community questions. Occasionally, we may include motivational messages to inspire our audience, because content creation is a challenging endeavour.

Is there an existing creator you can draw inspiration from, offering similar passion or expertise, or from a business perspective in the same industry?
MasterClass

Analysis:
After comparing the highlights from our answers, we determined that we align most with the **Aggregators** category. This category emphasizes analysing and breaking down complex information, often incorporating commentary, visuals and text for better understanding.

Although we plan to occasionally include motivational messages, this will not be our primary focus. Therefore, we chose not to identify as **Gurus**.

CHAPTER 3
FINDING YOUR NICHE AND UNDERSTANDING THE CONTENT LANDSCAPE

You're now probably at the point where you are thinking, "Great, but how do I know what content to make? How do I get started, and who is my audience?" – they are the right questions to ask. To start you off, we have created a reflective exercise that draws from our experiences with brands and influencer audiences. Complete the exercise to define your own audience. We can't do it for you; we can only give you direction; every approach is unique.

To get you in the right reflective space, answer the three questions opposite as well as you can. Keep them in mind as you continue reading, and refine your answers at any time. To support you in getting started, we completed the exercise from our perspective as authors of this book. If you find it tricky to answer the questions, take a look at our example on page 40.

EXERCISE

What are you an expert in or passionate about?
(e.g. a specific craft, series, genre, or a profession like gardener or dentist)

_____

_____

Why do you want to create content?
(e.g., sales, PR, fame, talent acquisition, lead generation)

_____

_____

Who would you like to consume/see your content?
(This answer should relate to the previous question.)

_____

_____

EXAMPLE

What are you an expert in or passionate about?
We are experts in modern digital space content creation strategies for both individuals and companies, from both an influencer and corporate perspective.

Why do you want to create content?
We want to make people aware of our book content so we can help individuals get started on their new career path and help companies successfully adapt their online content to reach their goals.

Who would you like to consume your content?
We would like to engage with anyone who wants to create content and needs a guide about the journey, structure and direction. We want to support people and companies of all ages and industries, positions and goals.

Now that you have done that, let's dive right in.

How do you find an audience if you are just starting out?

Defining and building an audience might feel overwhelming. Here's how you can begin:

1. **START WITH A SMALL, FOCUSED NICHE**

   Don't stress about trying to reach everyone at once. Start by identifying a specific group of people who share a common interest or need. This ties back to your reflection question about who you'd like to consume your content. While that answer may initially be broad, it directly connects to your goal. You'll only reach the right audience when the people engaging with your content align with and support your goal. This is particularly crucial for established brands and influencers.

   If you're just starting out, you might be more flexible with your goals – or perhaps you haven't yet defined one. Chances are, your initial response is that you want to reach as many people as possible who are interested in your expertise or passion, to gain recognition or fame. As a starting point, that's fine, provided you adhere to the Ten Commandments and avoid creating content that just adds to the noise.

   So, how do you begin? By understanding your audience. If you're passionate about a specific topic (even if you're not a professional expert, like a lawyer or doctor), you're likely part of your own audience. For example, if sci-fi books are your passion, immerse yourself in online communities dedicated to that genre. Share content that resonates with their interests, and over time, you'll build an audience and discover the intersection between your passion and their engagement.

2. ENGAGE IN EXISTING COMMUNITIES

You can still learn from and engage with potential followers, even before your audience grows. Join forums, comment on related content and participate in discussions. This helps you get a sense of what people are looking for and how you can provide it.

3. EXPERIMENT AND LEARN

Your first few posts or videos don't need to be perfect. In fact, they're valuable opportunities to learn. Pay close attention to what resonates with your audience and what doesn't. Early feedback, even from a small group of viewers, can help refine your approach.

As a corporate marketer, you'll likely focus on specific engagement metrics and feedback from the audiences you've defined. Be prepared to adjust your content accordingly, even if it means losing engagement from a different group that initially interacted with your content.

As an influencer just starting out, you probably have more flexibility. You can follow the research steps outlined earlier, define your target audience and systematically analyse the response to your content, adjusting until you consistently reach the right people.

However, if you're still exploring and have expertise or a passion, remain open to potential audiences as long as you're able to produce a variety of content. Once you create a piece of content that generates significant engagement, focus on replicating that style and defining the audience it attracts.

To further support you in narrowing down and defining the content you'll create for your audience, we will introduce the three steps of the content definition pyramid. This tool is a key part of our content creation process.

When you have found your direction (niche, audience, goal) and are ready to move forward on your path, you need to know what to expect from the environment you and your audience are moving into. We call that environment the **content landscape**. The base of the pyramid is the content landscape, which is directly connected to the audience.

THE THREE STEPS CONTENT DEFINITION PYRAMID

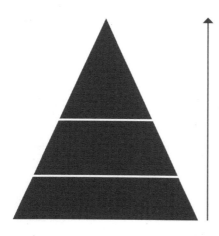

3. How and why should you fill the gap

2. Understand your gap

1. Understand your content landscape

In its simplest form we can define the content landscape as the entire ecosystem in which online content exists and evolves. Think of it as a digital environment that includes all the platforms, creators, trends, audiences and content types that shape what people consume. Imagine the content landscape as a giant map, with varying terrains where your content will exist.

STEP 1: UNDERSTAND YOUR CONTENT LANDSCAPE

This step involves looking at the current landscape and identifying what's already there – it's crucial to grasp the context and observe how content has evolved over time. You will need to analyse and identify the five key aspects relevant to your defined expertise and passion.

For instance, if a creator is successfully making TikTok videos focused on viral trends and dancing, you would not expect to see those videos on LinkedIn. Understanding the landscape means recognizing that the LinkedIn audience would not relate to such content, because the platform focuses on business, career development and knowledge sharing. Traditionally, LinkedIn is designed for polished, academic, written content. However, the landscape is dynamic. Since LinkedIn introduced video posts – which were expected to be high-quality – it has now evolved to include short video formats similar to YouTube Shorts.

This is where knowing your content landscape is crucial. The same video creator could adapt their content for LinkedIn by showcasing their dance skills while emphasizing their career as a dancer. This adaptation could appeal to LinkedIn's audience, if it aligns with the creator's original goal. For example, if the creator's goal is to generate leads for their dance studio, targeting a professional audience of aspiring dancers or individuals seeking to learn dancing could make sense.

However, all content possibilities should be driven by a clear strategy. Therefore, analysing your ideas against the content landscape should always be your first step, constantly circling back to those three questions.

Constantly monitoring and adapting to your landscape is key, as is anticipating changes. The landscape is continually evolving, so understanding prevailing trends will guide your entry into the content space.

To help you navigate, we have identified five key aspects that shape the content landscape:

1. PLATFORMS

These are the 'territories' where your content lives. Each social media platform has its own rules, formats and audience preferences. For instance, TikTok is known for short, engaging videos, while LinkedIn caters to professional, long-form content. Understanding the landscape of each platform helps you tailor your approach. Exploring the specifics of each platform's rules, formats and audience preferences could fill an entire book, but there are plenty of overviews and detailed analyses available online for you to consult.

2. CONTENT TYPES

This includes all the different formats of content – videos, blogs, podcasts, infographics, memes and more. Each type serves a unique purpose and appeals to different audiences across various platforms. For example, a meme might quickly go viral, but a podcast can establish long-term authority and trust. It's essential to choose a format that aligns both with the audience you've defined and the characteristics of your chosen platform.

3. ANTICIPATING TRENDS AND VIRALITY TO STAY AHEAD OF THE CURVE

Trends and virality are the waves that flow through the content landscape. Trends dictate what's popular at any given moment, from viral challenges to trending hashtags. Some trends are short-lived, while others evolve into cultural phenomena. Recognizing these waves early allows you to ride them effectively or even create your own.

As a beginner, it's often best to focus on one platform initially, or ensure that the platforms you're targeting share similar characteristics (e.g., short video formats). The key is understanding your audience so well that you can anticipate what will trend within their specific interests. Keep in mind that you should only engage in trends that help you achieve your objectives.

Recognizing trends is an art that seasoned marketers and successful influencers refine over time. It requires practice and active engagement across your targeted platforms. While developing this skill, here's what we recommend:

Monitor Platforms and Keep an Eye on Trendsetters:
Pay close attention to what early adopters, influencers and industry leaders are doing – they often spot trends before they blow up. Platforms like TikTok's 'For You' page or Instagram's Explore tab are excellent for identifying emerging patterns. Most platforms also provide creators with insight pages and analysis tools to track performance and spot opportunities.

Trends frequently originate within specific groups or platforms. For example, TikTok has established itself as a hub for viral content. Keep an eye on rising creators, new hashtags and trending audio. These early indicators can provide valuable insights into where momentum is building and help you stay ahead of the curve.

Use Trend Analysis Tools:
Tools like Google Trends or platform-specific Creative Centers can provide data on what's gaining momentum. Look for topics or formats that are spiking but haven't yet hit the mainstream.

Understand the Lifecycle of Trends:
Every trend follows a lifecycle – emergence, peak, saturation and decline. By observing how past trends

have evolved, you'll start to recognize the early signs of a new trend. When a trend feels fresh but hasn't reached mass adoption, that's your moment to jump in.

From a corporate marketing perspective, this might be more challenging due to lengthy approval processes. Therefore, establishing shorter approval cycles is crucial. Jumping on a trend too late can have the opposite effect of what you intended.

Don't Just Follow Trends – Experiment and Test:
Test your own ideas. Create pilot content and analyse its performance. Sometimes, your unique take on a topic, or even an entirely fresh concept, could spark the next big trend. The faster you experiment, the more likely you are to capitalize on emerging trends.

4. AUDIENCE BEHAVIOUR AND PREFERENCES

The audience is the 'climate' of your content landscape – it determines what flourishes and what doesn't. Understanding how audiences interact with content (e.g. Do they prefer short videos or long reads? Do they comment, share or just watch?) is crucial for crafting successful content.

You can determine this by studying which of your content pieces perform well or by closely observing the content of other creators who target the same audience. You can't really understand your audience unless you engage with the platforms they use.

For companies planning to launch on platforms like Instagram, your marketers need to extensively use these platforms themselves. Only by being active on the platforms you intend to leverage will you understand their dynamics. Without this understanding, no effective content strategy can emerge.

Follow competitor accounts or role model influencers in your niche. Analyse their engagement, read through comments and observe how their audience interacts with different types of content. Are viewers engaging more with longer instructional videos? Are certain themes, like self-improvement or nostalgia, resonating more? Understanding these preferences can help predict what content might perform well.

5. COMPETITION AND COLLABORATORS

Just as businesses have competitors, so do content creators. However, in this landscape, collaboration often plays a significant role. Co-creating with other influencers, jumping on shared trends or partnering with brands can amplify your reach. Knowing who operates in your space helps you differentiate yourself and find opportunities for collaboration.

Each element works together to inform your content strategy and ensure you're not just throwing meaningless, impactless content into the void.

Much like the business environment, the content landscape is dynamic. It shifts constantly based on audience preferences, technological advancements and cultural changes. But here's the catch: while business environments focus on markets, industries and competition, the content landscape zooms in on the digital world, examining how creators and brands interact with online audiences.

If you're producing highly polished, long-form videos on Instagram without realizing the platform favours Reels (short, engaging clips), your content might underperform. Conversely, recognizing that podcasts are gaining traction could help you tap into a growing audience that values in-depth conversations.

When stepping into the world of content creation, understanding the landscape is vital before embarking on the journey. Without this knowledge, you risk creating content in a vacuum, disconnected from what your audience actually wants and expects.

STEP 2: UNDERSTAND YOUR GAP

Step two involves identifying the gap you aim to fill. As Jeff The Car Company, you can't possibly create every type of car video for your social media. Instead, you need to pinpoint an unexplored niche in the market. Building on insights from the first step, your objective is to fill that gap and cater to either a niche or audience. Whether your goal is to outperform competitors or simply meet demand within that space, your content should resonate uniquely with your audience.

Let's walk through an example.

> Jeff The Car Company's (JCC) cars are full electric and sold in the affordable price range. JCC has identified young, environmentally conscious consumers as their primary audience. They've also analysed their audience's platform preferences and decided to focus on YouTube. Through research, they discovered that the most-watched and successful videos on car-related channels focus on driving experience comparisons, primarily of fuel-powered cars.
>
> After further brainstorming and online platform research with their main audience in mind, JCC's marketers identified an ongoing debate that drives community engagement in traditional driving experience videos. They noticed that comparison videos highlighting the one-tank distance of different cars

sparked significant community interaction. JCC wants to adapt this idea to their audience's interests.

By combining their audience knowledge and product expertise (electric cars) with the one-tank distance concept, JCC identified a gap: **Sustainable Automotive Practices and Innovations.** This gap was confirmed through a competitive content landscape analysis. Now, JCC's marketers must dive deeper into understanding this gap to capitalize on it effectively.

STEP 3: UNDERSTAND HOW TO FILL THE GAP

Now that JCC – and hopefully you – have identified a gap, step three focuses on understanding how and why you should fill it. This process ties directly back to your overarching goal. For example, what's the ultimate purpose of creating content for Jeff The Car Company? Is it to boost car sales or to alleviate post-purchase dissonance among customers?

Purchase dissonance refers to the unease customers may feel after making a purchase. Consider this scenario: you buy a car, but after driving it for a few days you find the experience unsatisfactory. Ideally, you want your customers to associate positive feelings with their purchase – imagining themselves driving confidently, feeling like a celebrity in their new car. The goal is to eliminate any negative feedback tied to the purchase.

JCC's marketers must define their content creation objectives in alignment with their gap and goal. JCC's analysis revealed their goal: to boost car sales. Their research showed that young, cost-conscious customers often encounter negative perceptions of electric cars, such as their limited range and frequent need for recharging.

By conducting a thorough content landscape analysis, JCC's marketers identified that their target audience – environmentally and cost-conscious young drivers – mainly consumes car-related content on YouTube and TikTok. They also found that the most engaging car content aligns closely with their product and the gap identified in step 2.

To address this, JCC decided to educate their potential customers by showcasing economical driving styles that maximize an electric car's battery range. These driving tips not only extend battery life but also reduce charging costs, addressing their audience's need for affordability.

JCC also realized that this content doesn't currently exist. They noted that the most successful videos in this space, though focused on fuel-powered cars, often followed a vlog-review style and typically showcased driving experiences along predefined routes.

Based on this insight, JCC's marketers decided to create short videos highlighting economical driving tips while

CHAPTER 3
FINDING YOUR NICHE AND UNDERSTANDING THE CONTENT LANDSCAPE

maximizing battery range. Each video would feature a different scenic route, with a competitive element of trying to break JCC's previous distance record.

Moving forward, the key is to ensure that every piece of content is crafted with the audience in mind.

Before diving into the next chapter, you may have questions about how to implement these strategies. Reflect on the content in this chapter with the following exercise. Then, move on to **The Ten How-Tos in Content Creation**, which will prepare you for the chapter on **Crafting Superior Value for Your Audience**.

EXERCISE

Take your time as you work through the following three steps. Reflect on what you want and need to do with your content creation platform of choice.

1. **Understand Your Landscape**
   - What do you know about your audience's online behaviour?
   - What platforms are you considering for your content?
   - Have you found creators producing similar content?
   - What format do you envision for your content, and is it consumed by your target audience?

   _____
   _____
   _____
   _____
   _____
   _____
   _____

CHAPTER 3
FINDING YOUR NICHE AND UNDERSTANDING THE CONTENT LANDSCAPE

2. Understand Your Gap
- Is there a type of content you believe is missing or under-served?
- If so, can you fill that gap?

_____

_____

_____

_____

_____

3. How and Why Should You Fill That Gap?

_____

_____

_____

_____

_____

CHAPTER 4

THE TEN HOW-TOS IN CONTENT CREATION

Before moving on to how you craft value for your audience and create content of superior quality, here are answers to the ten most frequently asked questions we've received from fellow content creators in the corporate and influencer spaces. These 'How-Tos' will guide you in confidently navigating your content creation journey.

1. HOW DO I EFFECTIVELY CHOOSE WHICH SOCIAL MEDIA PLATFORM TO PROMOTE AND DISTRIBUTE MY CONTENT?

Identify where your audience spends their time. Each platform has its own strengths – Instagram for visuals, TikTok for short-form videos, YouTube for longer content, and LinkedIn for professional networking. Match your content to the platform's format, but avoid overextending yourself. Start with one or two platforms that align with your goals. Continuously monitor platform developments, as platform characteristics and audience expectations often change (LinkedIn now includes short-form scrollable videos).

2. HOW DO I CHOOSE THE RIGHT NICHE FOR MY CONTENT CREATION JOURNEY?

Pick a niche you're passionate about that has a clear audience. Look for areas where your skills and interests overlap with market demand. Research your competition to identify gaps you can fill. For example, Alishquiche found success by focusing on movies,

TV shows and books – content that felt authentic to her while also meeting the interests of her audience.

3. HOW DO I CREATE ENGAGING AND COMPELLING CONTENT THAT RESONATES WITH MY TARGET AUDIENCE?

To create content that clicks with your audience, you need to have a good understanding of them. Study their interests, pain points and preferences. Authentic, valuable or entertaining content tends to perform best. Engage with your audience through comments or polls to get direct feedback. The more you refine your content based on what resonates, the stronger your connection will be.

4. HOW DO I OPTIMIZE MY CONTENT FOR SEARCH ENGINES AND INCREASE DISCOVERABILITY?

Apply SEO best practices like keyword research, relevant tags, and clear, engaging titles or captions. For platforms like YouTube, detailed video descriptions and attention-grabbing thumbnails are essential. On Instagram and TikTok, using strategic hashtags relevant to your audience and content can significantly boost discoverability. Consistency in your environment and format also helps algorithms recognize your content, increasing exposure to your target audience.

5. HOW DO I OVERCOME THE CHALLENGES OF BUILDING AN ONLINE PRESENCE AND GAINING FOLLOWERS?

Focus on consistency and quality. Post regularly and engage with your audience by responding to comments and messages. Collaborate with other creators, participate in trends, and join online communities in your niche. Building a following takes time, so be patient and prioritize delivering value over quick growth.

6. HOW DO I CHOOSE THE RIGHT EQUIPMENT AND SOFTWARE FOR CONTENT CREATION ON A BUDGET?

You don't need expensive gear to start. Many successful creators begin with just their smartphones and free editing tools like Canva or iMovie, AI enhanced editing apps. As your audience grows, invest in affordable tools like a ring light, microphone or entry-level camera. Upgrade your setup only when you really need it to enhance your content quality.

7. HOW DO I DEVELOP A CONSISTENT AND SUSTAINABLE CONTENT CREATION SCHEDULE?

Set realistic goals based on your time and energy. If daily posting feels overwhelming, start with a few posts per week. Use scheduling tools like Click-Up, Trello or Notion to organize ideas and deadlines. What matters most is finding a tool you're comfortable with. Consistency is more important than quantity, so establish a posting rhythm that fits your lifestyle, workload or goals, and stick with it.

8. HOW DO I MONETIZE MY CONTENT AS A CONTENT CREATOR?

There are several ways to monetize content, such as brand deals, sponsored posts, affiliate marketing, ad revenue or selling products. Start by building a loyal, engaged audience – brands value creators with strong, interactive followings. Experiment with different income streams, like launching exclusive content on Patreon, using affiliate links or selling merchandise. Focus on methods that complement your content and audience experience.

9. HOW DO I DEAL WITH CRITICISM AND NEGATIVE FEEDBACK CONSTRUCTIVELY?

Criticism is part of the content creation process, so learn to distinguish between constructive feedback and hate. Respond graciously to constructive criticism and use it to improve. Ignore or block hateful comments that bring no value. Build a strong sense of self and remember that not everyone will resonate with your content – and that's okay.

10. HOW DO I STAY INSPIRED AND MOTIVATED THROUGHOUT THE CONTENT CREATION JOURNEY?

Stay inspired by engaging with other creators, learning new skills and experimenting with fresh ideas. Take breaks when necessary to recharge your creativity. Set small, achievable goals to stay motivated, and celebrate your progress. Surround yourself with a supportive community that understands the ups and downs of content creation.

By addressing these common 'How-Tos', you will feel better equipped to navigate the ever-evolving world of content creation and are ready to move on to the next part: **Crafting Superior Value for Your Audience.**

CHAPTER 5

CRAFTING SUPERIOR VALUE FOR YOUR AUDIENCE

Now that you understand the framework of the content landscape, have conducted some necessary research for your content, and learned how to identify gaps, we can focus on what matters most: creating value – **superior value** – for your audience.

Some readers might wonder why this chapter wasn't placed first, given its importance. Here's the rationale: understanding the content landscape is foundational, but crafting value is where everything comes together. To create content that resonates, you must have a clear grasp of what your audience considers valuable. This chapter builds on the earlier framework, guiding you on how to leverage your understanding of the landscape to produce meaningful, impactful content.

Think of the earlier chapters as setting the stage – helping you to identify gaps and understand the context. Now, we're diving into the **how** of creating impactful content.

Whether you're Jeff The Car Company, an independent content creator, or an organization with a social media presence, the success of your content depends on the value it brings to your audience. Without value, your content becomes just another drop in an already overflowing ocean of noise.

But how do you craft value? What does 'value' mean in the context of content creation? Let's break it down into key principles that will guide you in developing content that resonates with your audience and keeps them engaged.

CHAPTER 5
CRAFTING SUPERIOR VALUE FOR YOUR AUDIENCE

1. KNOW YOUR AUDIENCE

The foundation of crafting valuable content starts with knowing your audience inside out. Creating superior value begins with deeply understanding their **needs, pain points, desires and interests**. You're not creating content for everyone – you're creating content for a specific group of people with particular problems, interests or goals.

The more precisely you can define your audience, the more tailored and effective your content. Many creators mistakenly believe that value comes from flashy production or high-tech equipment. In reality, **true value lies in solving your audience's problems or fulfilling their desires**. This requires focusing less on what you assume is valuable and more on what your audience truly **wants or needs**.

Building on the insights from the **Three-Step Content Definition Pyramid**, extend your analysis by asking yourself:
> Who am I speaking to?
> What are my audience's true needs, interests or problems?
> How can I help solve those problems or improve their lives?
> How can I make their lives easier, better or more enjoyable through my content?

For **Jeff The Car Company**, this might involve identifying distinct audience segments such as:
> **Car enthusiasts**: Interested in performance features, technical specifications and cutting-edge automotive technology.
> **Young, environmentally conscious first-time buyers**: Seeking cost-efficient, sustainable driving solutions.
> **Families**: Focused on safety ratings, space and reliability.

Each group has different priorities and concerns. Car enthusiasts may want detailed insights into performance metrics, while families prioritize safety features and space. Meanwhile, young buyers value environmentally friendly options paired with cost efficiency.

Your goal is to zero in on their specific desires and challenges. Their problems need solving and their needs must be addressed.

By deeply understanding and catering to these unique needs, you'll craft content that not only captures attention but also builds trust and loyalty.

Example: For Jason Big Muscles, a fitness influencer, superior value could come from creating workout plans for busy professionals that are both time-efficient and easy to follow. The challenges faced by this audience include limited time for exercise and an overwhelming amount of information in their daily lives.

Jason might include tips on maintaining motivation, staying consistent and finding time to work out despite a hectic schedule – these are real problems his audience faces, so solving them provides undeniable value.

2. PROVIDE USEFUL INFORMATION OR ENTERTAINMENT (IDEALLY, BOTH)

There are two types of value you can offer: **informational value** and **entertainment value**. The most successful content often strikes a balance between the two. People are drawn to content that either solves a problem, educates them or entertains them. The sweet spot is doing both at the same time.

> **Informational Value**: Offer your audience something they didn't previously know. This could be tips, tutorials or insider knowledge about your niche. For instance, Jeff The Car Company could create videos that explain how to find the best deals on new electric vehicles, or uncover cheap charging spots. This type of content empowers people with knowledge, making them feel informed and confident in their decisions.

> **Entertainment Value**: The key here is to be engaging, relatable or humorous when appropriate (a luxury brand might not benefit from a comedic approach). Jeff The Car Company could create lighthearted skits about the humorous side of car shopping or share behind-the-scenes footage from their dealership. When content is enjoyable, it keeps viewers coming back for more.

3. BUILD TRUST THROUGH CONSISTENCY AND AUTHENTICITY

In the digital world, trust is everything. You want your audience to view you as a reliable source of information, entertainment or insight. The two pillars of trust are **consistency** and **authenticity**.

> **Consistency**: Irregular posting makes it difficult to maintain an engaged audience. People need to know what to expect from you and when. Develop a content schedule that works for you, whether it's weekly videos, daily posts or monthly updates. For example, Jeff The Car Company might post car reviews every Monday or car maintenance tips every Wednesday. Consistency shows your audience that you are committed and dependable.

> **Authenticity**: Audiences can spot inauthenticity a mile away. They want to connect with a real person, not a faceless brand looking to make a sale. Be transparent about your intentions, processes, and even your mistakes. Jeff The Car Company could share real customer stories or talk about challenges they've faced in the industry. Authenticity builds relationships that go beyond transactions.

4. ENGAGE DIRECTLY WITH YOUR AUDIENCE

The internet is not a one-way street. Content creation in the digital age is a **conversation** between you and your audience. People appreciate feeling heard and valued, so engage with them directly. Respond to comments, ask questions and involve your audience in the content creation process.

For Jeff The Car Company, this could mean asking viewers what kind of car-related tips they'd like to see next or hosting a live Q&A to answer questions about car buying. By engaging directly, you're not just delivering content – you're building a community.

5. OFFER MORE THAN JUST CONTENT: PROVIDE SOLUTIONS

While the end goal for many businesses is to sell products or services, your content should never feel like an endless sales pitch. People don't want to feel constantly sold to; they just want solutions to their problems.

Superior value means going beyond surface-level content to offer real, actionable solutions. People are bombarded with information every day, but they truly **appreciate clear steps and useful insights**.

For example:
> **Harley326**, a TikTok dance influencer, creates beginner tutorials. To provide superior value, she could break down common mistakes beginners make and offer step-by-step guides for improving specific skills. Sharing personal stories about her own struggles as a beginner would also make her content relatable and inspiring.

Jeff The Car Company could create content that helps potential buyers make decisions, such as:
> A buyer's guide comparing electric cars to gas cars.
> How to trade in your old car for maximum value.
> Choosing the best family car based on safety and space needs.

By offering specific, solution-based content, you establish yourself as a trusted resource, increasing audience engagement and loyalty.

Not Every Creator Focuses on Practical Solutions – And That's Okay

If your primary focus is entertainment – such as day-in-the-life vlogs, comedy skits, or lifestyle content – **superior value still matters.** In these cases, value comes from the emotional impact and connection you create with your audience.
> **Day-in-the-Life Vloggers:** Your value lies in offering viewers a glimpse into your world. Whether it's showcasing a unique routine, humorously tackling daily chores or sharing

relatable content, the value comes from fostering a sense of connection and belonging.
> **Comedy Creators**: Your value is in making people laugh. By providing moments of joy and lightheartedness, you give your audience an escape from daily stress – an incredibly valuable service.

Even if you're not solving practical problems, you're still fulfilling a deep need: for inspiration, entertainment, belonging or emotional connection.

6. CREATE CONTENT THAT EMOTIONALLY RESONATES

A key aspect of providing superior value is connecting with your audience on an emotional level. Whether you're inspiring them, making them laugh or helping them overcome fear or doubt, building an emotional bond strengthens your relationship. Creators who focus on providing solutions and information can greatly enrich their content by ensuring it resonates emotionally.

Take **Jason Big Muscles** as an example: Instead of solely focusing on the technical aspects of working out, he could share motivational stories, as well as struggles from his own fitness journey and how he overcame them. This relatability helps his followers see that they can overcome obstacles. By building emotional connections, Jason not only offers fitness tips but also serves as a source of inspiration and motivation.

Similarly, **Harley326** could connect with her beginner audience by showing vulnerability – posting videos of her own dance fails or documenting her journey as she learns challenging new moves. This demonstrates to her followers that perfection isn't necessary to start dancing and that everyone experiences growth through practice.

7. ADAPT AND EVOLVE

Creating superior value isn't a one-time task – it requires ongoing improvement and innovation. The digital content world evolves rapidly; what works today may not work tomorrow. Audience preferences shift, platforms introduce new features, trends emerge or fade, and competitors continually raise the bar. To stay relevant, you must adapt and evolve, constantly refining your content and finding fresh ways to provide value.

This involves:
> **Listening to feedback**: Regularly engage with your audience to learn what they enjoy, what they don't and what they'd like to see more of.
> **Analysing trends**: Stay updated on industry trends to ensure your content remains timely and relevant.
> **Experimenting**: Don't shy away from trying new formats or exploring topics slightly outside your usual niche. Experimenting can lead to unexpected opportunities to deliver even more value.

For **Jeff The Car Company**, this might mean adapting content style to align with current trends. If TikTok users are leaning towards short, snappy clips, Jeff's team could experiment with concise, engaging videos. If long-form content makes a comeback, they could shift to producing in-depth car reviews. Jeff's initial strategy on YouTube might have focused on comprehensive car reviews, but staying flexible allows them to pivot based on audience demand and platform trends.

8. **BUILD A COMMUNITY AROUND YOUR CONTENT**
Superior value extends beyond the content itself – it's also about creating a **community** where your audience feels connected to you and each other. A sense of belonging fosters loyalty, and people who feel part of a community are more likely to remain engaged over time.

For instance, **Harley326** could encourage her followers to share videos of themselves participating in her dance challenges, fostering a community where dancers can motivate and support one another. She might even feature fan submissions or host live events to further strengthen these connections.

Jeff The Car Company could build community by creating a Facebook group or forum for first-time car buyers, where they can ask questions, share experiences and seek advice. This transforms JCC's content from mere information to an interactive resource that supports the audience throughout their buying journey.

Jason Big Muscles could ask his followers to share their fitness struggles, success stories or progress photos related to his workout plans. By spotlighting these stories, he motivates his community and reinforces the impact of his content.

CRAFTING VALUE: THE KEY TO LONG-TERM SUCCESS

Creating value for your audience goes beyond simply publishing content. It's about understanding who you're speaking to, addressing their needs, and building genuine relationships through consistency, authenticity and engagement. When you provide information and entertainment while staying flexible and responsive to your audience's needs, you'll craft content that resonates and drives lasting success.

As you progress on your content creation journey, keep these principles in mind. If you need a refresher on identifying your audience, revisit **Chapter 3**. Every piece of content – post, video or blog – should have your audience's needs at its core. When you craft content with value, the results – engagement, community growth, and even sales – will naturally follow.

EXERCISE

Take a moment to reflect and answer the following questions:

Who is your target audience, and what specific problems or needs can you address through your content?

_____

_____

_____

_____

What type of value (informational, entertainment, both) do you currently provide, and how can it be enhanced to better engage your audience?

_____

_____

_____

_____

_____

CHAPTER 5
CRAFTING SUPERIOR VALUE FOR YOUR AUDIENCE

How can you build trust with your audience through consistent and authentic content creation?

_____

_____

_____

_____

What strategies can you implement to directly engage and involve your audience with your content, making them feel part of a community?

_____

_____

_____

_____

_____

CHAPTER 6
NAVIGATING YOUR POSITIONING

After crafting valuable content for your audience, the next crucial step is positioning yourself in the online world and maintaining consistent messaging. **Positioning** defines how you stand out from competitors and helps your audience understand why they should engage with your content.

Positioning isn't just about follower counts or views – it's about identifying the unique value you bring and understanding where you fit in the content landscape. Creators like Casey Neistat and Liza Koshy enjoy considerable success, although they may not have the same reach as PewDiePie. These differences in reach don't necessarily correlate with financial success, highlighting the importance of defining your goals and filling specific market gaps.

1. DEFINING YOUR UNIQUE VALUE PROPOSITION (UVP)

Your **UVP** summarizes the value you offer, the audience you serve and what sets you apart. Let's look at three examples:

- **Jeff The Car Company**: "We help first-time car buyers find great deals and make confident decisions by simplifying the car-buying process."
- **Harley326**, an aspiring TikToker: "I create fun, relatable dance challenges for beginners, with tips to improve your moves."
- **Jason Big Muscles**, a fitness influencer: "I help busy professionals build muscle with efficient, no-nonsense workouts."

Each UVP reflects what makes these creators unique. Your UVP should answer three key questions:
- **Who are you serving?**
- **What problem are you solving?**
- **How are you different from competitors?**

2. STAY WITHIN YOUR IDENTIFIED NICHE

Your **niche** is a focused segment of the broader market, allowing you to stand out by serving a specific audience.
- **Jeff The Car Company** could focus on electric vehicles or first-time buyers.
- **Harley326** targets beginner dancers looking to improve their skills.
- **Jason Big Muscles** is for busy professionals seeking quick, efficient fitness routines.

By narrowing your focus, you'll be able to serve your audience more effectively and increase your impact.

3. CRAFTING YOUR BRAND VOICE AND PERSONALITY

Your brand's voice and tone shape how your audience perceives you.
- **Jeff The Car Company** adopts a friendly, approachable tone to ease first-time buyers' concerns.
- **Harley326** uses a fun, energetic style to connect with young beginner dancers.
- **Jason Big Muscles** uses a motivational, straightforward tone to reach busy professionals.

Consistency in your voice builds trust and recognition, and reinforces your brand identity.

4. POSITIONING AGAINST COMPETITORS

Understanding your competitors is essential for effective positioning. Identify what makes you different and highlight those qualities:

> **Jeff The Car Company** positions itself as an educational advisor rather than just a dealership pushing car sales.
> **Harley326** appeals specifically to beginners, filling a gap where many dance influencers focus on advanced techniques.
> **Jason Big Muscles** offers quick, no-frills workouts for busy professionals, contrasting with influencers who promote lengthy, intensive sessions.

Throughout your content creation process, ask yourself: **What gaps do I want to fill? How and why should I fill those gaps?**

Success isn't determined solely by subscriber count. Factors such as your audience's socioeconomic status, the total potential audience size and the gaps you address all play significant roles.

5. COMMUNICATING YOUR POSITIONING

Once you've defined your UVP and niche, it's crucial to communicate your positioning clearly across all platforms. Your bio, tagline and content should consistently reflect your unique value:

> **Jeff The Car Company**: "Simplifying car-buying for first-time buyers."
> **Harley326**: "Dance challenges for beginners – let's have fun and improve together!"
> **Jason Big Muscles**: "Quick, effective workouts for busy people."

These concise statements immediately convey your focus and value proposition.

6. FINANCIAL GOALS AND SUCCESS METRICS

Success in content creation isn't just about followers and views; it's about aligning with your specific goals.

For **Jeff The Car Company**, success might mean attracting more followers from the right demographic (first-time buyers) and tracking how many engage with car-buying resources.

For **Jason Big Muscles**, success could be measured and tracked by the number of followers purchasing his workout programs or engaging with affiliate links.

Even with a smaller subscriber count, financial success can come through affiliate marketing, sponsored posts or product sales. Define your success metrics – whether financial growth, audience engagement or impact – and align your content strategy accordingly.

Whether your goal is maximizing earnings, making an impact or simply entertaining your audience, your UVP, niche and voice shape your journey. Every creator's approach is unique, but success comes from navigating your positioning and defining your goals.

As you refine your content strategy, continually ask yourself: **How can I uniquely serve my audience?**

By standing out in an increasingly competitive space, you'll position yourself for long-term success.

EXERCISE

Take a moment to reflect on the following questions:

1. **What unique value do you offer your audience, and how does it differentiate you from your competitors?**

   _____

   _____

   _____

2. **What specific niche or gap in the market can you focus on to serve your audience more effectively and stand out from the crowd?**

   _____

   _____

   _____

3. **How will you measure your success — through financial growth, audience engagement or impact — and what steps can you take to align your content with those goals?**

   _____

   _____

   _____

CHAPTER 7

FOLLOWER DISSONANCE

Content creators who may experience audience growth, will face more challenges than merely producing content. One of the most significant hurdles is follower dissonance – the gap between what your followers expect and what you deliver. This disconnect can lead to misunderstandings, disengagement and a decline in your audience's interest.

1. WHAT IS FOLLOWER DISSONANCE?

Follower dissonance, **much like purchase dissonance in marketing**, occurs when there's a disconnect between the content a creator initially offered and the content they provide over time. This misalignment can leave followers feeling dissatisfied, confused or disengaged. For creators, it often results in a plateau in growth and a lack of clarity as to why their audience is no longer engaging.

Imagine following a creator for specific content – such as dance videos, fitness tips or car reviews – only to see them pivot to unrelated material like political commentary or personal rants. This disparity between expectations and reality creates dissonance, gradually eroding the follower's interest and commitment.

While following someone doesn't involve a monetary transaction, it does require a subconscious **investment** – most notably, **time. In today's world, time is one of the most valuable resources, even more so than money, because once spent, it cannot be recovered.** This is why the phrase "time well spent" underscores the relationship between time and value. As a creator, if you fail to meet your audience's expectations, they may feel their time has been wasted, leading to dissonance and disengagement.

2. WHY ENGAGEMENT MATTERS MORE THAN FOLLOWER COUNT

It's far more important to prioritize **audience engagement and satisfaction** than to focus solely on follower count. The real measure of success isn't how many followers you accumulate, but how well you serve, engage and sustain the attention of those followers.

Followers invest their time in consuming your content, and it's your responsibility to ensure that time is well spent. This means catering to their needs, solving their problems, or entertaining them in ways that align with your original value proposition.

For example, Jeff The Car Company might build a loyal following based on informative content about affordable cars. However, if Jeff suddenly shifts focus to luxury vehicles without addressing the needs of his budget-conscious followers, he risks creating dissonance. Even if he attracts new luxury buyers, he could lose his core audience in the process. Success doesn't come from merely gaining more followers but from **serving your audience consistently and effectively**, ensuring their expectations are met with each piece of content.

3. STRATEGIES TO PREVENT FOLLOWER DISSONANCE

One of the most effective ways to prevent follower dissonance is to actively solicit **feedback** from your audience. By understanding their preferences and evolving your content based on their input, you can avoid straying too far from what originally attracted them.

For instance, if one of Jeff The Car Company's videos on affordable cars goes viral and garners significant positive feedback, Jeff could create a recurring series on budget-friendly car-buying tips. This keeps the content relevant and maintains audience engagement.

Similarly, Harley326, the TikTok dancer, might face dissonance if she abruptly switches from beginner-friendly dance challenges to political commentary. Even if she's passionate about her new focus, her audience, who followed her for fun dance content, may feel alienated. To maintain loyalty, Harley should either introduce new content gradually or find ways to connect her original dance material to any new directions.

By **staying true to your core content** while exploring new areas in a way that remains relevant to your audience, you can minimize the risk of alienating followers.

CHAPTER 7
FOLLOWER DISSONANCE

4. REALIGNING WITH YOUR AUDIENCE

If you notice signs of follower dissonance – such as reduced engagement, negative feedback, or a drop in follower count – it's essential to take steps **to realign with your audience**. Start by reviewing past successes: What types of content have resonated most? By doubling down on these, you can rebuild your connection.

For example, Jason Big Muscles may attract followers for his quick, efficient workout routines. If he suddenly posts longer, more complex fitness content without a proper transition, his audience might disengage. Jason could resolve this by gradually introducing longer workouts while continuing to offer shorter routines, catering to both existing and new followers.

Similarly, Jeff The Car Company could explore luxury car reviews without alienating budget-conscious buyers, by maintaining content tailored to first-time buyers. This dual strategy ensures all segments of their audience feel valued.

5. WHEN IT'S OKAY TO LOSE FOLLOWERS

Sometimes, follower dissonance is unavoidable, especially when evolving your content. Not every follower will stay on your journey, and that's okay. Growth often requires change, and some followers may not align with your new direction.

PewDiePie experienced this. As he transitioned from gaming content to commentary, he lost some followers but gained a new, more aligned audience. **Losing followers doesn't equate to failure**; it often signifies evolution. Those who truly resonate with your vision will stay.

For instance, if Harley326 decides to focus on advanced dance techniques instead of beginner tutorials, she may lose her original audience of beginners. However, this new direction will attract a more aligned, advanced audience.

For Jeff The Car Company, shifting towards luxury vehicles may alienate budget-conscious buyers, but if the goal is to target high-end customers, this transition aligns with their strategy. As long as Jeff remains consistent with his new focus, they will attract the right followers for their niche.

6. STAYING TRUE TO YOUR BRAND AND VISION

Follower dissonance often arises when creators stray too far from their core identity in an attempt to please everyone. While it's important to be mindful of your audience, it's equally crucial to stay aligned with your goals and values.

EXERCISE

Ask yourself:

Am I staying true to my vision, or am I veering off course to satisfy temporary trends?

_____

_____

_____

_____

_____

What is the core message or value I want to share, and is my content consistently reflecting that?

_____

_____

_____

_____

_____

For Jason Big Muscles, if his mission is to help busy professionals get fit with minimal time investment, he should continue offering practical, no-nonsense advice – even if some followers seek more detailed or advanced content. By staying true to his mission, he will attract the right followers for his brand.

Some creators will feel trapped by their original niche, fearing that any deviation will alienate their audience. However, staying true doesn't mean being rigid. Authenticity involves evolving alongside your audience while ensuring your content reflects your passions. If Jason finds a new passion for detailed, long-form fitness content, he shouldn't feel forced to stick to short-format workouts. The key is transitioning thoughtfully and bringing his audience along for the ride.

KEY QUESTIONS FOR CREATORS:

- Am I staying true to my evolving vision?
- Does my content still reflect my core values and goals?
- Am I enjoying the process of creating this content?

Follower dissonance is a natural part of growth, but it can be managed with attention to audience expectations, consistent messaging and clear communication. Instead of focusing solely on follower count, **prioritize engagement and serving your audience's needs.** This fosters deeper connections and loyalty.

By staying true to your brand, gathering feedback and adapting your content thoughtfully, you can minimize dissonance and strengthen your bond with your community. Ultimately, this commitment will lead to sustained success and tangible results.

CHAPTER 8

KEY LESSONS IN ENTREPRENEURIAL THINKING

Becoming a successful influencer or content creator requires adopting the mindset of an entrepreneur. As a creator, you're not just responsible for engaging content; you're building a personal brand, identifying revenue streams and sustaining long-term growth. Incorporating entrepreneurial concepts like **effectuation and bootstrapping, and principles such as the Bird-in-Hand, Affordable Loss, and Worldview Control vs. Prediction** can be the difference between fleeting fame and a lasting, profitable career.

Here are the key entrepreneurial lessons every content creator should adopt to thrive in today's digital landscape:

1. THOU SHALT TREAT THYSELF AS A BRAND

Successful creators view themselves as brands, strategically aligning their content with long-term goals. This aligns with the **Bird-in-Hand** principle, which encourages starting with the resources and identity you already possess.

Everything you post contributes to your brand identity. Ask yourself:

> **Who am I and what can I immediately offer my audience with the resources I have?**

Example: Kim Kardashian leveraged her existing network and visibility to build a multifaceted empire. Starting as a reality TV star, she consistently evolved her brand into a global powerhouse.

2. DIVERSIFY YOUR REVENUE STREAMS

Relying solely on ad revenue or sponsorships can be risky. Explore multiple income streams, such as merchandise and affiliate marketing, or launching your own products. **Bootstrapping** – reinvesting your earnings – helps you grow your business without external funding.

Apply the **Affordable Loss** principle: focus on opportunities where the risk is manageable.

Example: Lilly Singh expanded from YouTube into a late-night show, book authorship and live tours. While her ventures showcase diversification, they also highlight the risks of expanding into new areas and reaching new audiences who may not know her original content – these new audiences may not be as familiar or welcoming. Her late-night show faced heavy criticism and was cancelled after two seasons.

Is diversification worth it? Diversification is essential but not a guaranteed path to acclaim. Prepare for potential setbacks, learn and adapt. Balance bold moves with calculated risks to grow sustainably.

3. UNDERSTAND YOUR MARKET (EFFECTUATION IN ACTION)

Knowing your audience is key, and this is where **effectuation** – using available resources and working flexibly – comes in. The **Bird-in-Hand** principle within effectuation urges creators to leverage their existing resources (niche audience, skills or themes) to seize opportunities.

Worldview Control vs. Prediction is another important concept: instead of trying to predict how the market will change, control what you can by focusing on what's within your immediate grasp, such as your content strategy, engagement and resources. Entrepreneurs who practice this don't wait for trends – they create them.

Start with what you know, who you know and what you have. Don't wait for the perfect opportunity or trend to emerge. Instead, focus on how your current resources can serve your audience today and create new opportunities in the future.

Example: MrBeast began with simple gaming videos, reinvesting early revenue into ambitious projects. Instead of chasing trends, he leaned into high-stakes challenges and viral moments based on what he had access to.

4. THINK LONG-TERM

Entrepreneurs think beyond short-term gains. Content creators should adopt this mindset, focusing on actions that contribute to sustainable, long-term growth.

In planning for the future, use **Affordable Loss** to manage risk – invest only what you can afford to lose, keeping your vision intact.

Example: Viral moments are thrilling but short-lived. Creators like Emma Chamberlain built their brands through authenticity, allowing for steady, long-term growth that supports ventures like her coffee line and podcast. Emma's focus on genuine engagement reflects her commitment to a lasting brand.

5. CREATE SOLUTIONS, NOT JUST CONTENT

Entrepreneurs aim to solve problems. For content creators, this means offering more than engagement – providing real value, whether educational, entertaining or inspiring.

Ask yourself, what problem does my content solve? Is it teaching something new? Is it making people laugh or inspiring them to act? Every piece of content should offer something more than just engagement – it should deliver real value.

Example: Marie Forleo grew her following by addressing entrepreneurs' struggles through practical advice, actionable insights and motivational content, transforming her audience's challenges into learning moments.

6. BUILD RELATIONSHIPS, NOT JUST FOLLOWERS

Entrepreneurs know that relationships, not just transactions, fuel success. Content creators should engage genuinely with their audience and collaborators.

Example: Gary Vaynerchuk (GaryVee) is known for his personal engagement with followers, showing his dedication to community. His consistent connection-building has earned him a fiercely loyal audience.

7. EMBRACE FAILURE AND LEARN FROM IT

Failure is part of the entrepreneurial journey. Using the **Affordable Loss** approach allows creators to take risks they can afford while learning from failures, both big and small.

It's also critical to acknowledge that failure in content creation includes online criticism and bullying, not just flops. Being a content creator means stepping into a highly visible role, which can attract negativity. Trolls and critics often exploit moments of vulnerability, making the experience of failure more personal and painful. This is a mental game, and not everyone is prepared for the intensity of public scrutiny that comes with being online. Aspiring creators need to build resilience and develop strategies to manage this aspect of failure.

Embrace failure as a part of the journey. Experiment with new ideas and be open to change but manage your risk by focusing on what you can afford to lose. Prepare yourself mentally for the challenges of public visibility. Learn from your failures, adjust your strategy and keep moving forward.

Example: Lilly Singh took a mental health break. In her YouTube video "I'll see you soon ...", she addressed how she was mentally, physically and spiritually exhausted from producing content daily for over eight years. The importance of mental health and taking breaks shows that content creation is a real hustle. She managed her break well because she transparently shared with her community her struggles, and clearly communicated that she would return after a break. She took the lessons from her experiences, adapted her approach to take care of her mental health, and continues to evolve, using both successes and failures as stepping stones for growth.

8. NETWORK LIKE AN ENTREPRENEUR

Networking is essential. Building relationships with other creators, brands and industry professionals can open doors to new opportunities and collaborations.

Example: Charli D'Amelio leveraged connections with TikTokers, YouTubers and major brands to expand her reach and boost her brand. Partnerships with big names like Dunkin' Donuts show how networking can elevate a creator's profile.

9. STAY AGILE AND PIVOT WHEN NEEDED

Entrepreneurs excel in adaptability, adjusting strategies as markets evolve. Content creators need this same agility to stay relevant. Don't hesitate to change direction if engagement dips or new opportunities arise.

Example: PewDiePie pivoted from gaming to commentary, maintaining relevance in a shifting YouTube landscape. His willingness to adapt has kept him at the top of the platform.

10. THOU SHALT MONETIZE THY INFLUENCE

Creators must think about profitability. **Worldview Control** emphasizes focusing on areas of control, like income streams, over future uncertainties. Choose partnerships, affiliate marketing and endorsements that align with your brand.

Example: Patricia Bright, a beauty YouTuber, is selective with brand collaborations, ensuring they resonate with her audience. By prioritizing authenticity, she's created a sustainable income while staying true to her brand.

Becoming a successful content creator goes beyond posting – it requires the mindset of an entrepreneur; resilience and the willingness to evolve. By viewing yourself as a brand, diversifying income, thinking long-term and adapting to challenges, you can create a thriving, sustainable career in the digital landscape.

CHAPTER 9

PUSH VS PULL: STRATEGICALLY REACHING YOUR AUDIENCE

As a content creator, one of the most important challenges is figuring out how to grow and engage your audience. Whether you're just starting out or looking to scale your following, leveraging both push and pull marketing strategies can significantly amplify your reach. Each approach plays a vital role in how you attract, engage and retain your audience. Understanding when and how to use both strategies will help you maximize growth and keep your community engaged long-term.

In this chapter, we'll explore how you, a content creator, can use push and pull marketing to grow your following, build your brand and create meaningful connections with your audience.

1. WHAT IS PUSH MARKETING FOR CONTENT CREATORS?

Push marketing is when you actively push your content or message in front of an audience. This means you are taking deliberate actions to reach potential followers, whether through paid promotions, collaborations or targeted outreach. You are putting your content directly in front of people who may not have heard of you before and encouraging them to engage.

Push marketing is especially useful when you want to get fast results or reach a wider audience quickly.

Examples of Push Marketing for Content Creators:
> **Paid social media ads**: Running ads on platforms like Instagram, TikTok or YouTube to promote a new video or post.
> **Collaborations with other creators**: Partnering with other influencers to introduce your content to their audience.
> **Giveaways and contests**: Creating contests that require participants to follow, like or comment to enter.

Example 1: Jason Big Muscles wants to rapidly grow his audience. Jason decides to use push marketing by running targeted Instagram ads promoting his new 30-day fitness challenge. He creates eye-catching video ads showing his short but intense workouts and directs viewers to sign up for the challenge via his website.

In addition, Jason collaborates with another fitness creator who has a similar audience but focuses on nutrition. Together, they do a live workout session on Instagram, cross-promoting their brands. This exposes Jason to a new audience, bringing in followers from his collaborator's fanbase.

Example 2: Harley326 is looking to grow her following beyond the beginner niche. She uses push marketing by partnering with a popular TikTok influencer who focuses on viral dance trends. They create a duet where Harley adds her beginner-friendly spin to a popular dance. This partnership helps her reach a wider audience, including more advanced dancers, who might appreciate her unique take on choreography.

Harley also promotes a TikTok ad targeting users interested in dance challenges. The ad highlights her approachable tutorials, inviting users to follow her for easy-to-learn dances.

2. WHAT IS PULL MARKETING FOR CONTENT CREATORS?

Pull marketing is an inbound approach where you create content that naturally draws people to your platform. Instead of pushing your message out to people, you focus on creating valuable, entertaining or educational content that your audience actively seeks. The goal of pull marketing is to attract an audience organically by offering value that resonates with their interests.

Pull marketing often takes longer to yield results but gradually builds stronger, more engaged communities. It focuses on creating a lasting relationship with your followers through consistent, valuable content.

Examples of Pull Marketing for Content Creators:
› **SEO-optimized content**: Writing blog posts or creating YouTube videos that are optimized for search so that people find your content when they're looking for specific topics.

> **Educational or tutorial videos**: Creating content that teaches your audience something valuable (e.g. a "How to Get Fit in 20 Minutes a Day" video).
> **Organic social media engagement**: Posting consistently on platforms like TikTok or Instagram and interacting with followers in the comments or through Q&A sessions.

Example 1: While Jason is using push marketing to rapidly grow his audience, he knows that pull marketing is key to building a long-term community. Jason creates a YouTube channel full of SEO-optimized workout tutorials. His videos, such as "10-Minute Morning Workout for Busy Professionals" or "How to Build Muscle with Limited Time," are tailored to attract his target audience – people who are actively searching for ways to get fit quickly.

He also writes blog posts on his website that offer fitness tips and guides, optimized to rank high on Google searches for fitness advice for busy professionals. These pieces of content naturally pull in an audience, who are looking for solutions to their fitness challenges.

Example 2: Harley326 knows that pull marketing will help her build a loyal following on TikTok. Instead of just doing trending dance challenges, she also creates evergreen content like "Beginner's Guide to TikTok Dances" and "5 Tips to Improve Your Dancing in 10 Minutes." These videos provide lasting value to her audience, especially new users who are looking for easy ways to get started with TikTok dances.

Harley also engages her followers by asking them to suggest dance challenges in the comments, fostering a deeper connection and interaction with her community. Her content is not only entertaining but also educational, making people feel they are learning something new while having fun.

3. PUSH VS. PULL MARKETING AS A CONTENT CREATOR

Knowing when to use push or pull marketing depends on your goals and your stage of growth as a creator.

We recommend you use Push Marketing when:
- You're launching a new product, challenge or piece of content and need quick awareness.
- You want to reach new audiences.
- You have a time-sensitive offer, like a limited-edition merchandise drop or a live event.

Example: Jason Big Muscles is launching a paid fitness course, so he uses push marketing by running Facebook and Instagram ads targeted at professionals looking for workout solutions. This allows him to quickly reach a new audience and drive immediate sign-ups.

Use Pull Marketing when:
- You want to build a loyal, engaged community.
- Your focus is on creating long-term value through consistent, educational or entertaining content.
- You're aiming for organic growth by attracting followers who actively seek out your content.

Example: Harley326 focuses on pull marketing by regularly posting engaging dance tutorials on TikTok. She interacts with her followers through comments, asking them for feedback on what dances they'd like to learn next. This keeps her audience engaged, builds a community around her brand, and encourages followers to return to her page.

4. COMBINING PUSH AND PULL FOR MAXIMUM IMPACT

The most successful content creators know that the real magic happens when you combine push and pull marketing strategies. By using both approaches, you can maximize your reach while building deeper relationships with your audience.

Example: Jason uses push marketing by running ads for his new 30-day fitness challenge, driving immediate sign-ups. At the same time, he uses pull marketing by consistently posting YouTube tutorials and workout guides that are optimized for SEO. His ads create quick bursts of traffic, while his organic content sustains long-term engagement with his audience.

Example: Harley326's push strategy includes collaborating with popular TikTokers to expose her content to a wider audience. Simultaneously, her pull strategy involves creating evergreen dance tutorials that continue to attract new followers. The collaboration brings in new followers, while her consistent content keeps them engaged.

5. BUILDING A PULL STRATEGY FOR LONG-TERM GROWTH

If your goal is to build a community that supports your brand over the long term, pull marketing is the foundation. By focusing on valuable, engaging content, you can naturally attract people to your platform and keep them coming back for more.

KEY PULL STRATEGIES FOR CREATORS:

- **Evergreen content**: Create tutorials or educational content that remains relevant long after you post them.
- **Engagement**: Encourage your audience to comment, ask questions and share your content. The more involved they are, the more loyal they will become.
- **Consistency**: Post regularly and show up for your audience with fresh content. Consistency builds trust and keeps your followers engaged.

While pull marketing builds long-term engagement, push marketing can help accelerate your growth when you need to reach a new audience or promote something specific. As a content creator, mastering the balance between push and pull marketing is key to building a thriving online presence. Push marketing allows you to reach new audiences quickly and drive immediate engagement, while pull marketing creates lasting relationships and long-term loyalty. By strategically combining both approaches, you can grow your following, engage your audience and build a brand that lasts.

EXERCISE

Think about your own current content creation needs. **Do you need to reach a new audience or promote something specific? Or is your goal to build a community that supports your brand over the long term?**

CHAPTER 9
PUSH VS PULL: STRATEGICALLY REACHING YOUR AUDIENCE

Identify three potential push or/and pull strategies you could use to achieve your desired outcome for your brand:

_____

_____

_____

_____

_____

_____

_____

_____

_____

_____

_____

_____

_____

CHAPTER 10

CRAFTING EFFECTIVE ADVERTISEMENTS — BRAND DEALS

Picture this: You're growing. Your followers are climbing, your views are picking up, and then it happens – you get approached by a brand that wants to work with you. The brand explains the process, guiding you through their expectations, and you deliver your first branded video asset.

It's an exciting milestone, but it's also a pivotal moment that requires a clear understanding of the responsibilities on both sides. Based on our extensive experience working with first-time influencers and collaborating with brands, we've outlined key considerations to help you successfully navigate your first brand deal. There's a checklist at the end of this chapter.

HANDLING YOUR FIRST APPROACH OR BRAND DEAL: A GUIDE FOR ASPIRING CONTENT CREATORS

Navigating your first brand deal can feel both exciting and overwhelming. It's a milestone that signals your content is making an impact. However, without guidance, it's easy to take missteps that could affect your reputation or earnings. Here's a roadmap to help you approach your first brand collaboration with confidence:

1. UNDERSTAND PROFESSIONALISM: WHAT BRANDS EXPECT FROM YOU

For many young creators, especially those who haven't worked in corporate environments, the concept of professionalism may feel distant. Professionalism is critical in brand collaborations, and it will directly impact how you're perceived and whether you secure future deals.

Here's what professionalism means in the context of influencer work:
> **Timeliness**: Brands operate on tight schedules. Meeting deadlines for content submission and feedback is essential.
> **Clear Communication**: Respond promptly to emails or messages. Keep your tone respectful and professional, even if you're communicating informally.

> **Reliability**: Follow through on your commitments. If you promise to deliver specific content, ensure it meets the agreed-upon requirements.
> **Preparedness for Feedback**: Brands may ask for revisions. Approach this with a collaborative mindset, rather than taking it as criticism of your creativity.

Why This Matters: Brands invest time and money in partnerships. Professionalism reassures them that their investment is in safe hands, making them more likely to work with you again.

2. ASSESS THE BRAND AND ITS VALUES

Before accepting any deal, ensure the brand aligns with your personal values and the interests of your audience. Collaborating with a brand that doesn't fit your niche or goes against your principles can lead to follower dissonance or backlash.

Key Questions to Ask Yourself:
> Does this brand align with my content and audience?
> Am I happy to personally use or endorse this product or service?
> How will my audience perceive this partnership?

For example, if your content focuses on sustainable living, partnering with a fast-fashion brand might undermine your credibility.

3. UNDERSTAND THE BRAND'S EXPECTATIONS

Clarify what the brand expects from you. These expectations might include:
- **Content Deliverables**: How many posts, videos or stories are required?
- **Content Format**: Are they looking for a review, tutorial or unboxing video?
- **Deadlines**: When do they need the content published?
- **Exclusivity Clauses**: Will you be restricted from working with competing brands?

Understanding these details upfront ensures you can meet their expectations and prevent miscommunication.

4. SET YOUR RATES AND NEGOTIATE CONFIDENTLY

Determining your rates can be daunting, especially if you're new.

Factors to Consider:
- **Follower Count and Engagement Rates**: Even micro-influencers (1,000–10,000 followers) can command strong rates if the engagement is high.
- **Content Quality**: High production value can justify higher rates.
- **Time Investment**: Consider the time required for shooting, editing and reviewing content.

Negotiation Tip: Brands expect some back-and-forth on pricing. Be prepared to explain why your rates are justified, and don't be afraid to counter an offer if you feel undervalued.

5. REQUEST A CONTRACT

A contract protects both you and the brand, ensuring clear expectations and legal security. Look for these key components in the agreement:

> **Payment Terms**: How much will you be paid and when?
> **Usage Rights**: Can the brand repurpose your content for ads or other platforms? If so, for how long?
> **Exclusivity Clauses**: Are you restricted from working with similar brands, and for how long?
> **Deliverables and Deadlines**: Clearly outline what you'll provide and when.

If the contract seems complex, consider consulting a legal professional, even for a quick review. This might seem like an extra cost, but it's worth it to protect your rights.

6. MAINTAIN CREATIVE CONTROL WHILE BEING OPEN TO FEEDBACK

While brands may have specific guidelines, your audience follows you for your unique voice and style. However, professionalism also means being open to brand feedback and ensuring the content aligns with their objectives.

Tips to Maintain Balance:
> Negotiate flexibility in how you present the product or service.
> Suggest ways to incorporate the brand's messaging naturally into your content.
> Approach feedback as a collaboration rather than a critique.

7. BE TRANSPARENT WITH YOUR AUDIENCE

Transparency is key to maintaining trust. Always disclose brand partnerships according to platform guidelines and legal requirements (e.g. using hashtags like #ad or #sponsored). Followers appreciate honesty and are more likely to engage positively with sponsored content when they know you're being upfront.

8. TRACK YOUR PERFORMANCE AND REPORT BACK

After the collaboration, track the performance of your sponsored content. Metrics like engagement rates, click-through rates and follower feedback can provide valuable insights.

Post-Campaign Reporting:
Share these results with the brand. Providing a post-campaign report demonstrates professionalism and helps build a long-term partnership.

9. EVALUATE AND LEARN FROM THE EXPERIENCE

Reflect on your first brand deal:
> **What Went Well?** Did the collaboration feel seamless, and was the brand easy to work with?
> **What Could Improve?** Were there challenges, such as unclear communication or tight deadlines?
> **Audience Response**: Did your followers engage positively with the sponsored content?

Use these insights to refine your approach for future deals.

10. BUILD LONG-TERM RELATIONSHIPS

Brands prefer working with creators they trust. If your first partnership goes well, follow up with the brand to express your interest in future collaborations. Building long-term relationships can lead to more opportunities and maybe even exclusive deals.

Final Thoughts: Your first brand deal is a significant milestone, but it's just the beginning. By approaching it with professionalism, clear communication and confidence, you'll set the foundation for a successful career. Remember, professionalism doesn't mean sacrificing creativity – it means respecting the brand's investment while staying true to your unique voice.

THE IMPORTANCE OF MONITORING INFLUENCER BEHAVIOUR: PROTECTING YOUR BRAND'S REPUTATION

When brands partner with influencers, they are not only investing in their reach and engagement, but also in their personal brand and public persona. However, many followers view influencers as a single, inseparable entity – their online personality and real-life actions blend into one. This perception means that any behaviour or action taken by an influencer can reflect directly on the brand they are associated with, either positively or negatively.

1. WHY MONITORING INFLUENCER BEHAVIOUR MATTERS

Once a brand partners with an influencer, their actions – both online and offline – become a part of the brand's extended identity. This association carries risks, as any controversy, scandal or even minor misstep by the influencer can lead to public backlash, impacting the brand's reputation.

Consider These Scenarios:
> **Positive Reflection**: An influencer engages in philanthropy or is praised for promoting important social causes. This positively impacts the brand, aligning it with values such as social responsibility.

> **Negative Reflection**: An influencer is caught engaging in unethical behaviour, makes controversial remarks, or acts in ways that go against societal norms. The brand risks being perceived as complicit or supportive of such behaviour, leading to potential boycotts or reputational damage.

2. UNDERSTANDING THE BLURRED LINES BETWEEN INFLUENCER AND BRAND

For followers, there's often no clear distinction between the influencer as an individual and the influencer as a brand representative. This phenomenon makes it critical for brands to understand that:

> **The Influencer's Actions are the Brand's Actions**: When influencers endorse a product, their followers view it as a personal recommendation. Consequently, any unrelated behaviour by the influencer can indirectly affect how the brand is perceived.

> **Influencers Shape Brand Perception**: An influencer's lifestyle, values and public behaviour contribute to how the brand they represent is perceived by the audience. This perception can either strengthen or undermine the brand's image.

For example: If Jeff The Car Company partners with an eco-conscious influencer, their reputation for sustainability could be enhanced. However, if that same influencer is later caught driving gas-guzzling cars, Jeff's brand could suffer by association, even if the partnership has ended.

3. PROACTIVE STEPS FOR BRANDS

To mitigate risks, brands must take a proactive approach when engaging influencers:

Conduct Thorough Vetting

Before partnering with an influencer, brands should conduct comprehensive background checks. This includes reviewing:
- Past content (social media posts, videos, interviews).
- Public interactions and statements.
- Associations with other brands or organizations.

Ensure the influencer's values align with your brand's mission and ethos.

Set Clear Behaviour Expectations

Incorporate clauses into contracts that outline expected behaviour and consequences for actions that could harm the brand's image. These could include:
- Avoiding controversial topics unless previously agreed upon.
- Maintaining a professional tone and approach in all public engagements.
- Complying with specific codes of conduct.

Monitor Ongoing Activity

Even after a partnership is established, brands must actively monitor the influencer's activity:
- Regularly review their social media posts, comments and interactions.

- Stay alert to news or controversies involving the influencer.
- Use social listening tools to gauge public sentiment about the influencer and their association with your brand.

Have a Crisis Management Plan
Despite best efforts, situations may arise where an influencer's actions negatively impact your brand. Prepare for such scenarios by having a crisis management plan in place:
- **Quickly Address the Issue**: Acknowledge the situation and distance your brand from any harmful behaviour if necessary.
- **Communicate Clearly**: Issue statements that reaffirm your brand's values and clarify your stance.
- **End the Partnership if Needed**: In severe cases, it may be necessary to terminate the partnership to protect your brand's reputation.

Strike a Balance Between Trust and Oversight
While monitoring is essential, it's also important not to stifle the influencer's creative freedom. Influencers thrive on authenticity, and overly restrictive control can lead to content that feels forced or disingenuous and ends up alienating the audience.

Build Trust: Choose influencers who naturally align with your brand's values, to reduce the need for excessive oversight. Foster open communication, encouraging influencers to share their ideas while staying within brand guidelines.

Maintain Oversight Without Micromanaging: Focus on providing clear, upfront expectations rather than constant corrections. Periodically review content plans and key messages to ensure alignment.

5. BALANCING RISK AND REWARD

Partnering with influencers is a powerful strategy for expanding brand reach and credibility. However, the partnership is only as strong as the influencer's personal brand. By investing time in proper vetting, setting clear expectations and maintaining a watchful yet balanced oversight, brands can safeguard their reputation while reaping the benefits of influencer collaborations.

In the dynamic and fast-paced world of social media, ensuring your brand is associated with the right influencers is crucial. A proactive approach will help you navigate the risks, protect your image and build long-lasting partnerships that drive success.

Exercise: Prepare for Managing Multiple Brand Deals
Before diving into strategies for simultaneously managing multiple brand deals, it's crucial to understand the expectations and responsibilities from both sides of the partnership. We've crafted detailed checklists tailored specifically for influencers and brands. These checklists highlight essential elements that can make

or break a successful collaboration. Carefully review each point and take note of any that are new or unfamiliar. Mastering these aspects is key to building strong, mutually beneficial partnerships that drive results for both parties.

Influencer Checklist for Working with Brands:
1. **Understand the Brand's Goals**
   » Ask the brand to clarify the campaign's main objective: Is it to raise awareness, drive engagement, boost sales or promote a specific product?
   » Tailor your content to align with these goals while maintaining your unique style.

2. **Maintain Authenticity**
   » Ensure that the brand's product or service aligns with your values and interests.
   » Only promote products you genuinely believe in to maintain audience trust.

3. **Align Content with Audience Expectations**
   » Your audience follows you for a reason – don't alienate them by creating content that feels out of place.
   » Integrate the brand's product naturally into your usual content style (e.g., vlogs, tutorials, or Q&A).

4. **Review the Brand Brief Carefully**
   » Understand the brand's key messages, preferred tone and required content formats.
   » Take note of specific instructions like hashtags, call-to-actions (CTAs), or disclaimers (e.g., #ad, #sponsored).

5. **Set Clear Boundaries**
   » Discuss and agree on what you're comfortable promoting and how the product will be integrated.
   » Make sure you retain creative control to avoid content that feels overly scripted.

6. **Communicate Regularly with the Brand**
   » Establish a feedback loop. Share draft content early to ensure alignment.
   » Be proactive about updating the brand on your progress and timelines.

7. **Meet Deadlines**
   » Stick to agreed timelines to ensure the brand can meet its campaign schedule.
   » If unforeseen delays arise, communicate them immediately and early.

8. **Track and Share Performance Metrics**
   » Provide post-campaign performance reports, including metrics like reach, impressions, engagement rates, click-through rates and conversions.

» This transparency helps brands gauge the campaign's success and builds trust for future collaborations.

9. **Understand Legal and Financial Aspects**
    » Carefully review contracts to understand payment terms, content ownership and usage rights (e.g., can the brand reuse your content on their platforms?).
    » Discuss terms around exclusivity and ensure you're fairly compensated for any restrictions.

10. **Protect Your Mental Health**
    » Manage your workload to avoid burnout, especially when juggling multiple brand deals.
    » Set aside time for content planning, creation and personal breaks to sustain long-term creativity.

Brand Checklist for Working with Influencers:
1. **Research the Influencer's Audience**
    » Review the influencer's demographics, engagement rates and content style to ensure their audience aligns with your target market.
    » Analyse past collaborations to gauge their effectiveness in promoting similar products.

2. **Clarify Campaign Goals**
    » Clearly define the campaign's objectives: brand awareness, audience engagement, lead generation or direct sales.
    » Share these goals upfront to align with expectations.

3. **Provide a Detailed Brief**
   - » Include essential campaign details:
     - Key messages
     - Content guidelines (e.g., tone, style, must-mention features)
     - Deliverables (e.g., Instagram posts, TikToks, YouTube videos)
     - Deadlines
   - » Be specific but leave room for the influencer's creative input.

4. **Allow for Creative Freedom**
   - » Remember, influencers know their audience best. Trust them to present your product in a way that feels natural and engaging.
   - » Avoid micromanaging or demanding rigid adherence to a script.

5. **Set Clear Expectations**
   - » Outline deliverables, performance metrics and timelines explicitly in the brief.
   - » Specify any mandatory elements, such as hashtags, captions or calls to action.

6. **Maintain Open Communication**
   - » Be accessible for feedback and questions. This ensures a smooth collaboration process.
   - » Schedule regular check-ins, especially for long-term partnerships.

7. **Monitor the Influencer's Broader Activities**
   - » Keep an eye on the influencer's personal and professional behaviour – followers often perceive influencers and their associated brands as one entity, so any controversies could reflect negatively on your brand.

8. **Track Campaign Performance**
   - » Analyse data from the influencer's content (e.g., reach, engagement, conversions) to measure the campaign's success.
   - » Use this information to refine future campaigns.

9. **Establish a Long-Term Relationship**
   - » Build rapport with high-performing influencers to foster loyalty and create consistent partnerships – long-term collaborations often result in more authentic and impactful content.

10. **Protect Your Brand's Reputation**
    - » Develop a crisis management plan in case of negative feedback or controversies involving the influencer.
    - » Be prepared to address issues swiftly and transparently to minimize reputational damage.

MANAGING OVERFLOW WHILE DELIVERING QUALITY

You're doing well. Handling one project at a time was manageable, but now imagine five more companies reaching out. Suddenly, you're juggling multiple brand deals. A few months into this new phase, you might find that coming up with fresh, engaging ideas while maintaining your authenticity isn't as simple anymore. A good advertiser isn't just someone who creates the best ad – it's someone who can create the best ads *by Tuesday*.

As an advertiser myself, and with my co-author, Alishquiche, who works with perhaps more brands than any other Swiss creator, we've learned a few things about consistently generating fresh ideas and delivering high-quality ads. Here's our advice on how to never run out of ideas and how to continue crafting effective advertisements that align with your voice and your audience.

1. UNDERSTAND THE ADVERTISING OBJECTIVE
When embarking on a brand deal, it's essential to understand the type of advertisement you're expected to create. Different objectives require different approaches. Before brainstorming, ask yourself:
> **What does the brand want to achieve?**
> **Is the goal to inform the audience about a new product, persuade them to take action or remind them about the brand?**

CHAPTER 10
CRAFTING EFFECTIVE ADVERTISEMENTS – BRAND DEALS

For example, an informative ad introducing a new product will look very different from a persuasive ad pushing for a quick sale. The tone, message and even format will depend on the objective.

Brands will typically provide a brief, but as a content creator, it's your responsibility to ensure the brand's message aligns with your content style and your audience's expectations. This balance is crucial for creating authentic ads that resonate.

Example: Imagine Jeff The Car Company partners with an electric vehicle charger brand. If the goal is to inform, Jeff might create a video highlighting the charger's key features, such as its international availability and extensive network. If the goal is persuasion, Jeff could produce content showcasing the charger in action during a family road trip, emphasizing its speed and ease of use. By tailoring the ad to the brand's objective while maintaining Jeff's unique storytelling style, the message lands authentically.

2. MATCH THE BRAND'S OBJECTIVES WITH YOUR AUTHENTIC VOICE

Here's where things get tricky. Your audience follows you for your authenticity and unique voice. The best advertisements seamlessly integrate into your existing content.

Example: Jason, a fitness influencer, lands a deal with a meal prep company. His audience values quick, effective solutions. Instead of delivering a generic endorsement, Jason showcases how the meals fit into his daily routine: *"Here's how I save time and still hit my macros."* This approach aligns with Jason's voice and maintains trust with his audience.

Sometimes, brands may provide overly rigid briefs. If the brief doesn't allow flexibility, remind the brand that your authentic voice is why your audience trusts you. Work collaboratively to adapt the message for your platform.

3. **KEEP IDEAS FLOWING WITH CREATIVE PROCESSES**
   Managing multiple brand deals means the pressure to deliver new content is constant. Creativity isn't just about having brilliant ideas – it's about having a process that generates ideas consistently.

   Here's some ways we've managed in the past:
   - **Brainstorm in batches**: Dedicate time to generate ideas for multiple brands at once. Often, one campaign's concept can inspire another.
   - **Leverage your audience**: Read comments and direct messages. What do your followers enjoy? What questions do they frequently ask? Use this feedback to guide your content.

> **Tell stories**: Don't just showcase the product; embed it within a relatable narrative. Personal stories make the product feel more organic and less like a sales pitch.
> **Stay on top of trends**: Monitor viral challenges, dances or memes. Consider how you can creatively incorporate the product into current trends.

4. ENTERTAINMENT AND ENGAGEMENT OVER PURE PROMOTION

Audiences today can easily skip or scroll past ads. To grab attention, your content must entertain, educate or inspire. Great advertisements create value beyond promotion.

Example: Think about brands like Dunkin' or Red Bull. Instead of straightforward product showcases, Dunkin' collaborates with influencers to produce funny, relatable content. Red Bull aligns its branding with adventure sports, portraying its product as a lifestyle choice.

Here's how you can apply these principles:
> **Incorporate the product naturally**: Focus on the lifestyle, benefits or emotions associated with the product.
> **Engage your audience**: Run polls or host live Q&A sessions about the product. The more involved your audience feels, the more engaged they'll be.

5. EXPERIMENT WITH FORMATS

To keep your content exciting, even when working with multiple brands, try different formats.

Creative Formats to Try:
- **Behind-the-scenes content**: Show how the product integrates into your daily life.
- **Tutorials or how-tos**: Provide step-by-step guides about how to use the product.
- **Challenges**: Create challenges around the product and encourage your audience to participate.
- **Collaborations**: Partner with other creators for fun, interactive content that introduces the product to a wider audience.

Example: Harley326 is promoting wireless earbuds. Instead of saying, *"These earbuds have great sound,"* she creates a dance series demonstrating how the earbuds stay secure during intense moves. This high-energy approach showcases the product's benefits while staying true to her style.

6. DELIVER ADS ON TIME, EVERY TIME

Reliability is key. Brands often operate on tight schedules, and your ability to deliver high-quality content promptly can set you apart.

A great advertiser isn't someone who waits for inspiration – they're someone who can produce effective content consistently and meet deadlines. By understanding the brand's objectives early and maintaining a solid creative process, you'll avoid last-minute stress and deliver quality ads on time.

7. MAINTAIN AUTHENTICITY WHILE GROWING

The biggest challenge content creators face when working with brands is maintaining their authenticity. As you grow, you'll be approached by more brands, and it might be tempting to take every deal that comes your way. **But remember: your audience follows you for your unique voice, not for the ads.** If you start promoting products that don't align with your content or values, you risk losing their trust.

Before accepting a deal, ask yourself:
> **Does this product align with my content and audience?**
> **Can I create an ad that feels genuine and authentic?**

IN SUMMARY

Successfully managing multiple brand deals requires balancing creativity, authenticity and strategic alignment with brand objectives. By crafting ads that entertain, inform and stay true to your voice, you'll maintain audience trust while delivering impactful results for your partners.

CHAPTER 11

NAVIGATING THE ART OF NATIVE ADVERTISING

This chapter is designed for business owners and marketers aiming to harness influencer marketing effectively. Native advertising – where ads are seamlessly integrated into the platform and influencer content – is a crucial strategy for achieving impactful campaigns. Let's break down the essential elements of mastering native advertising.

1. PLATFORM-SPECIFIC CONTENT AND ADAPTATION, NOT REPLICATION

What works on one platform doesn't always translate well to another. Native advertising requires creating content specifically tailored to the unique audience and features of each platform. The digital advertising landscape changes rapidly, and what works today might not work tomorrow. Different platforms prioritize different types of content, and their algorithms are constantly evolving.

Example: Jason Big Muscles' quick, snappy workout videos are perfect for TikTok's fast-paced, attention-grabbing environment. However, on YouTube, those same workouts would need more depth, perhaps including detailed explanations or longer workout routines. Similarly, Harley326 can't just repost her TikTok dance videos to Instagram without modification. Instead, she might create Reels that align with Instagram's aesthetic and user expectations. Harley could shift her focus from Stories to Reels, if Reels gain traction, and Jason might explore live workout sessions if YouTube's algorithm starts to favour live content.

Always craft content that fits the platform you're using. Understand its format, algorithms, audience preferences to maximize engagement and relevance, ensure to stay updated on changes to maintain relevance and effectiveness.

2. AUTHENTICITY IN NATIVE ADVERTISING

Native advertising thrives on authenticity. The best campaigns feel like an organic part of the influencer's daily content. When done right, the audience barely notices the line between regular content and advertisements.

Example: Dunkin' Donuts successfully partnered with Charli D'Amelio by integrating their product naturally into her content. Instead of a traditional ad, Charli simply shared her love for Dunkin's drinks, which resonated with her audience. Likewise, Jason Big Muscles could feature a fitness product in his daily workout videos as a natural part of his routine, rather than delivering a scripted, forced promotion.

Ensure the product fits seamlessly into the influencer's content. Authenticity builds trust, which translates into higher engagement and better campaign results.

3. CREATIVITY AND TECHNOLOGY

While AI and other tech tools can help streamline the content creation process, native advertising depends on creativity. Tools can handle routine tasks like video editing, caption generation or analytics tracking, but it's the creative storytelling that truly connects with audiences.

Example: Alishquiche uses technology to automate tasks, but her real focus is on crafting engaging narratives. In her partnership with Oreo, she hosted a giveaway featuring a retro-themed Oreo Pac-Man arcade game machine. She invited her followers to share their favorite retro games in the comments and follow both her and Oreo's Switzerland account. This not only promoted the brand but also fostered a sense of community, aligning perfectly with her nostalgic, entertainment-focused content.

Leverage technology to support your workflow, but always prioritize creativity and storytelling to authentically engage and inspire your audience.

4. EMBRACING HOMOPHILY FOR EFFECTIVE ENGAGEMENT

A key concept to consider in content creation and audience engagement is **homophily** – the tendency for individuals to bond with others who are like them. Understanding this principle allows both creators and businesses to tailor their content to resonate with specific audience segments.

Creators should stay true to themselves while being mindful of their audience's preferences and interests. Similarly, businesses must select representatives who embody the brand's values and appeal to the desired demographic. By fostering a sense of homophily, both creators and businesses can cultivate loyal communities around their content. Be proactive in learning and adapting. Stay flexible and willing to pivot your strategy in response to new trends and platform shifts.

Native advertising isn't a static endeavour; it's an ongoing process of adaptation, creativity and authenticity. By tailoring your content to each platform, maintaining a natural integration of products, and staying informed about the latest trends, you can maximize the impact of your campaigns. Whether you're a marketer or an influencer, mastering these principles will ensure that your native advertisements not only resonate, but also drive meaningful results.

CHAPTER 12
CREATIVE BLOCK

Creative blocks are a common challenge in content creation, whether you're crafting advertisements for brands or generating fresh ideas for your own content. It's easy to feel stuck when the pressure is on to consistently produce high-quality work. This chapter will break down strategies to overcome creative block in two key areas:
1. Overcoming creative block when coming up with ideas for ads for brands
2. Overcoming creative block when creating your own content

OVERCOMING CREATIVE BLOCK WHEN COMING UP WITH IDEAS FOR ADS FOR BRANDS

When working with brands, the pressure to deliver engaging, on-brand content can lead to creative paralysis. Each brand has its own vision, and translating that into authentic, compelling content can feel daunting. Here's how you can navigate through this challenge:

1. USE PROVEN CREATIVE EXECUTION STYLES

A structured approach to ideation can help break through creative block. One of the most effective ways to generate ideas for brand ads is to tap into creative execution styles. These are well-established methods for delivering a brand's message in a way that resonates with the audience.

Here are seven styles to consider:
- **Part of Life**: Showcase the product in everyday situations. For example, if Harley326 is working with a sneaker brand, she could show how the shoes fit into her daily dance practice, making the product a natural part of her content.
- **Lifestyle**: Highlight aspirational aspects of the product. Jason Big Muscles might promote a luxury fitness tracker by showing how it enhances his workout routines and personal fitness goals, appealing to his audience's aspirations for self-improvement.
- **Fantasy**: Engage your audience with imaginative scenarios. Harley could create a fun, fantasy-inspired dance video where a brand's product gives her the edge in a futuristic dance-off.
- **Mood/Image**: Create content that evokes emotion. Jason could create a visually striking video focusing on the mood of strength and resilience, tying it to a fitness supplement he's promoting.
- **Musical**: Use music or rhythm to enhance the message. Harley could incorporate a brand into a viral dance challenge, driving engagement through entertainment.
- **Technical Expertise**: Demonstrate the product's features. Jason might create a detailed demonstration of a new fitness gadget, showcasing how it tracks his workout progress.
- **Scientific Evidence**: Present data or testimonials to support the product. Harley could share how a specific dance shoe improves performance, using data or customer feedback to validate the brand's claims.

2. ADAPT IDEAS FOR DIFFERENT PLATFORMS

Not every ad concept works across every platform. What works on Instagram may not perform well on TikTok or YouTube. It's important to tailor your ideas to the platform and its audience.

For example, Jason Big Muscles might create a quick, high-energy workout clip for TikTok that grabs attention in the first few seconds, while on YouTube, he might need to dive deeper into explaining the product's benefits in a longer format. Similarly, Harley326 might experiment with short dance tutorials on Instagram Reels, while on TikTok, she could use trends and challenges to more casually incorporate brand products.

3. BALANCE BRAND REQUIREMENTS WITH YOUR CREATIVE VOICE

When creating ads for brands, it's crucial to maintain authenticity. Your audience follows you for your unique voice, and ads should reflect that. Don't force an ad to fit the brand's vision if it feels disconnected from your style. Instead, find a way to integrate the product in a way that feels true to your content.

For example, Harley could promote a new set of headphones by incorporating them into her dance routine. Instead of making the ad about the headphones, she focuses on the performance, with the headphones naturally playing a part. This way, the product feels like an extension of her content rather than a forced plug.

CHAPTER 12
CREATIVE BLOCK

OVERCOMING CREATIVE BLOCK FOR YOUR OWN CONTENT

While ads come with brand guidelines, creating content for your own audience has its own set of challenges. Staying relevant and consistently engaging can lead to creative burnout.

Here are some ways to reignite inspiration when you're feeling stuck:

1. USE YOUR AUDIENCE AS INSPIRATION

Your audience is one of your greatest resources for content ideas. Pay attention to their comments, questions and feedback. They'll often tell you what they want to see, which can spark new ideas.

For example, if Jason Big Muscles notices his followers asking how he stays motivated, he could turn that into a series of motivational workout videos. Similarly, Harley326 could run a Q&A dance session based on her followers' requests, allowing her audience to shape the content she creates.

Listen to your audience. They'll guide you towards the content they want.

2. EXPERIMENT WITH CREATIVE EXECUTION STYLES

When you're feeling stuck, experimenting with different content styles can help you break out of a creative rut. Just as you use creative execution styles for ads, you can apply these styles to your own content.

For example, Harley could create a Slice of Life video showing a day in her life as a professional dancer, or Jason could craft a Mood/Image video focusing on the emotional journey of fitness and personal growth.

By trying new styles, you can keep your content fresh and exciting for your audience.

3. STAY CURRENT WITH TRENDS

Trends on social media evolve rapidly, and staying on top of them can inspire new content ideas. Aligning your content with popular challenges or formats can not only provide inspiration but also boost your engagement.

For example, if there's a trending fitness challenge, Jason could participate and add his own spin to it. If a viral dance is doing the rounds, Harley could adapt it into her tutorials. The key is to put your unique twist on these trends, to keep your content relevant and engaging.

4. GIVE YOURSELF A BREAK

When creative block hits hard, sometimes the best solution is to step back. Taking a break allows your mind to reset, helping you return with fresh energy and new ideas. Forcing creativity often leads to uninspired content, so give yourself permission to recharge.

Creative blocks are inevitable, whether you're working on ads for brands or creating content for your own audience. The key to overcoming them is to have a structured approach.

For ads, rely on proven creative execution styles and adapt your content to the platform. For your own content, listen to your audience, experiment with different styles and stay current with trends. By using these strategies, you'll not only overcome creative block but also produce content that resonates with your audience and keeps them engaged.

EXERCISE

Have you ever experienced a creative block? How did you overcome it? If not, imagine what you would do.

CHAPTER 12
CREATIVE BLOCK

Thinking about the seven styles, create an idea for each one based on your brand.

CHAPTER 13

THE SIX-STEP APPROACH TO CULTIVATING FANS

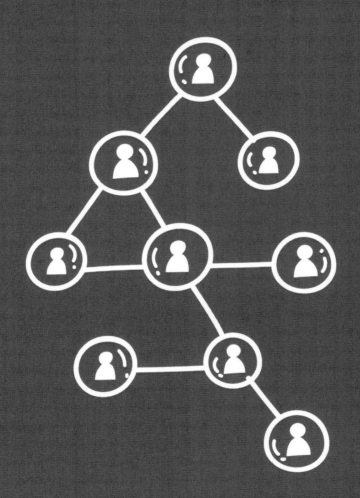

In this chapter, we explore the essential steps to transforming a community of followers into a dedicated fanbase. Whether you're a content creator or a brand, fostering engagement, loyalty and meaningful connections is critical to long-term success. Here's a detailed guide to building and maintaining a thriving fanbase.

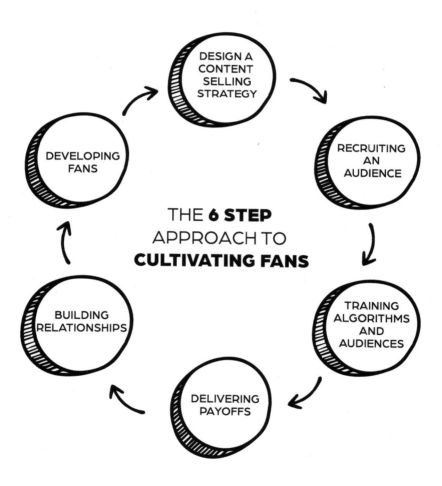

STEP 1: DESIGNING STRATEGY

The cornerstone of any successful content journey is a well-defined strategy. Whether you're an individual creator or part of a brand team, start by outlining your goals, identifying your target audience and mapping out your content creation process. Clarify your posting frequency and establish clear roles and responsibilities if you're working with a team. A solid strategy aligns your efforts with your long-term objectives, setting the stage for sustainable growth.

STEP 2: RECRUITING YOUR AUDIENCE

Once your strategy is in place, the next step is attracting and recruiting your audience. This involves selecting the right platforms, identifying visual themes, and crafting messaging that resonates with your target demographic. Think of your audience as a community – you want to inspire them to actively seek out and engage with your content.

Example: Lilly Singh built her audience on YouTube by sharing funny, relatable content about everyday life and cultural differences. Her humour and cultural insights resonated with both her South Asian roots and a wider audience, making her videos highly shareable, and helping her grow a massive, loyal following.

STEP 3: TRAINING ALGORITHMS AND AUDIENCES

To optimise content discoverability and engagement, it's crucial to train both algorithms and audiences. Algorithms prioritize consistent content, so establish regular posting schedules, maintain thematic consistency and use relevant tags or keywords to boost your content's visibility. Similarly, train your audience by setting clear expectations – whether it's weekly videos, daily stories or a monthly newsletter.

Example: PewDiePie became YouTube's most subscribed creator by consistently uploading content. His regular schedule and strategic use of keywords trained the platform's algorithm, while his audience came to anticipate daily uploads, boosting both visibility and engagement.

STEP 4: DELIVERING ON PAYOFFS

While consistency is vital, delivering value – what we call 'payoffs' – is equally important. Payoffs can take various forms, such as insightful information, behind-the-scenes content, entertainment or exclusive perks. Learn what resonates most with your audience and ensure you consistently deliver to keep them coming back for more.

Example: Casey Neistat built a loyal fanbase by offering high-quality vlogs that combined personal storytelling with cinematic filmmaking. His audience knew they could count on visually compelling, well-edited content, strengthening their connection with him.

STEP 5: BUILDING RELATIONSHIPS

Fan loyalty is rooted in authentic relationships. Engage in two-way communication by responding to comments, hosting polls or Q&As and actively seeking feedback. This humanizes your brand or persona, making your audience feel connected and valued.

Example: Gary Vaynerchuk is known for his tireless audience engagement. From replying to Instagram comments to hosting live Q&A sessions, Gary prioritizes building personal connections, fostering a fiercely loyal community of followers.

STEP 6: DEVELOPING FANS

The ultimate goal is to convert engaged followers into true fans—individuals who actively promote your content, participate in your community and advocate for your brand. By consistently providing value, nurturing relationships and fostering a sense of belonging, you can create a fanbase that supports and amplifies your growth.

Example: Emma Chamberlain has cultivated an exceptionally loyal fanbase by embracing her authentic, relatable personality. Her unscripted, casual content makes her audience feel like they're catching up with a close friend.

Emma's fans do more than watch her videos – they champion her brand. They share her content, purchase her merchandise and support ventures like her coffee line. A quick glance at the comments on her YouTube video *silly girl summer* reveals fans praising her authenticity and comparing her content to spending time with a friend. This deep connection transforms her viewers into true advocates.

By following these six steps, you'll not only attract followers but cultivate a dedicated fanbase that actively supports your growth. A fanbase built on trust, value and genuine connection is the foundation of lasting success, whether you're a content creator or a brand.

CHAPTER 14

MASTERING SOCIAL MEDIA: NAVIGATING ADVANTAGES AND CHALLENGES

This chapter is particularly aimed at business owners and marketers, but if you're a content creator, stick around – understanding the needs and strategies of brands can help you craft better brand deals and enhance your collaborations.

In today's fast-paced digital world, staying up-to-date with the ever-evolving landscape of social media marketing is crucial. With technology rapidly advancing, marketers and businesses must continually educate themselves to remain relevant, effective and competitive. Social media offers a vast array of opportunities, but it also comes with its own set of challenges that require careful navigation.

ADVANTAGES OF SOCIAL MEDIA MARKETING

Social media is a powerful tool for businesses, offering unparalleled opportunities for growth, engagement and brand visibility. Let's explore some key advantages:

1. **TARGETED AND PERSONALIZED ADVERTISING**
   One of the greatest strengths of social media is the ability to **target specific audiences** with personalized messaging. Platforms like Facebook, Instagram and TikTok allow businesses to segment their audience based on interests, behaviours and demographics.

Example Brand: Nike
Nike uses targeted ads on Instagram to reach people who have shown an interest in fitness, athletic apparel or specific sports. By tailoring its ads to a specific audience, Nike ensures its message reaches the right people at the right time, leading to higher engagement and conversion rates.

2. INTERACTIVE ENGAGEMENT
Social media provides a direct line of communication between brands and their audiences. Brands that engage in interactive, two-way communication foster a sense of community and loyalty.

Example Brand: Wendy's
Wendy's is famous for its witty and entertaining Twitter interactions. By roasting other brands, responding to customer tweets and joining trending conversations, Wendy's has built a loyal following that eagerly engages with its content. This sense of humour has set the brand apart and humanized its presence on social media.

3. REAL-TIME MARKETING AND CUSTOMER SERVICE
Social media allows brands to engage in **real-time marketing** and provide **instant customer service**. This is essential for building trust and responding to customer concerns quickly.

Example Brand: JetBlue
JetBlue is known for its fast, high-quality responses to customer questions and complaints on platforms like Twitter. Whether it's handling customer service issues or sharing flight updates, JetBlue has built a reputation for being responsive and attentive, enhancing its brand image and customer satisfaction.

4. LOW COSTS

Compared to traditional advertising methods, social media platforms offer affordable advertising options, making them accessible to businesses of all sizes.

Example Platform: TikTok
TikTok offers relatively low CPM (cost per thousand impressions) rates, allowing businesses to reach large audiences without spending heavily. This cost-effectiveness makes TikTok an appealing option for businesses looking to engage younger audiences and grow their brand without a massive advertising budget.

CHALLENGES OF SOCIAL MEDIA MARKETING

While social media offers many advantages, it also presents several challenges that businesses must navigate to succeed. Understanding these challenges is key to developing an effective strategy.

1. **USER-CONTROLLED ENVIRONMENT**
   Social media platforms are primarily user-driven, meaning that users have control over what they engage with and what they ignore. Brands must be cautious in how they approach advertising, ensuring their content is non-intrusive and adds value to the user experience.

   Users can easily skip or block ads, making it vital for brands to craft content that enhances the user-experience, rather than feeling like an interruption. Native ads or user-generated content often perform better because they seamlessly blend with organic content.

2. **AVOIDING IRRITATION**
   Pushing advertisements too aggressively can **irritate users** and create negative associations with the brand. It's important for businesses to strike a balance between promotion and engagement.

Excessive ad interruptions on platforms like YouTube or Apple TV have caused frustration among users, leading to ad blockers or negative feedback. Users expect a smooth experience, and constant ad bombardment can damage the brand's reputation.

3. RISKS OF HARMLESS CAMPAIGNS BACKFIRING

Even campaigns that seem harmless can backfire if not carefully thought out, potentially causing negative brand perception or public backlash. This is especially true when brands touch on sensitive social or political issues.

Example: Pepsi's Controversial Kendall Jenner Ad

The Pepsi ad featuring Kendall Jenner depicted a protest scene where Jenner leaves a modelling shoot, joins the crowd and offers a can of Pepsi to a police officer as a gesture of unity and peace. According to Pepsi, the ad was intended to position the brand as promoting harmony and understanding in a time of heightened social and political tensions.

However, the execution was widely criticised for trivialising serious social justice movements happening around the ad's release time, particularly Black Lives Matter. Critics argued it simplified and commodified complex struggles for racial equality and police reform. The imagery of Jenner handing a Pepsi to a police officer was seen as tone-deaf, suggesting systemic issues could be resolved with a soft drink.

The backlash stemmed from the ad's perceived insensitivity. It was seen as co-opting the visual language of protests – signs, chanting crowds and confrontations with police – without acknowledging the gravity or risks involved in real-world activism. For many, it reduced the serious fight for justice to a marketing gimmick, sparking outrage on social media.

HOW DID PEPSI RESPOND?
In response to the outcry, Pepsi quickly pulled the ad and issued a public apology, acknowledging that they had missed the mark. They expressed regret for any offence caused and committed to reviewing their internal processes to prevent similar missteps in future campaigns.

This incident highlights the importance of cultural sensitivity, thorough research, and understanding the content landscape when engaging with social issues. Brands must ensure their messaging aligns authentically with the values and experiences of their target audience. Consulting diverse perspectives during the creative process can help avoid blind spots that could lead to misinterpretation or backlash.

By understanding both the advantages and challenges of social media marketing, businesses and content creators can craft effective strategies that resonate with their target audiences while avoiding common pitfalls. The dynamic nature of social media requires marketers to stay informed and adaptable, ensuring they leverage its advantages while navigating its challenges with care and insight.

For content creators, recognizing these elements helps you understand what brands are looking for, allowing you to offer valuable, informed collaborations. By mastering the balance of engaging content and mindful marketing, you can thrive in the constantly evolving world of social media.

LET'S GO!
YOUR CONTENT CREATION JOURNEY AWAITS

As we reach the conclusion of this book, we hope our insights and advice have equipped you with the tools and confidence to thrive in your content creation journey. Whether you're a content creator or a business marketer, you can now navigate the dynamic world of content creation.

THE REALITY OF THE JOURNEY

Let's be real: content creation is not an easy path. It's a hustle that requires grit, perseverance and constant adaptation. There will be moments of doubt, creative blocks, and perhaps even times when you question your purpose. Not everyone will make it big. Success – however you define it – takes time.

But here's the good news: this book is your compass. Like any compass, it won't smooth out the terrain or eliminate obstacles, but it will point you in the right direction, helping you stay aligned with your goals at every stage of your journey. Whether you're starting out, facing a plateau or seeking to refine your strategy, this guide offers a framework to keep you moving forward.

REFLECT, APPLY, INNOVATE

Throughout this book, we've encouraged you to reflect on your goals, apply actionable strategies and embrace the creative process. Each chapter is designed to sharpen your understanding, from positioning and value creation to audience engagement and entrepreneurial thinking.

Now it's time to put everything into practice:

Content creators, use this guide as a springboard to create with purpose and authenticity. Let your personality shine and resonate with your audience, transforming followers into loyal fans.

Brands and marketers, leverage these strategies to forge meaningful collaborations and amplify your message while staying true to your core values.

In this ever-changing digital landscape, the only constant is change. Stay curious, remain adaptable and always seek to learn. Success isn't about chasing trends – it's about staying rooted in your purpose while growing alongside your audience.

Success in content creation is a journey, not a destination. There will be setbacks, but every failure is an opportunity to learn and adapt. Some days, you will feel lost in the wilderness, but remember: the compass needle always points towards your true direction. Trust the process, stay resilient, and focus on creating content that adds value.

STAY CONNECTED

We'd love to hear from you! Whether you have questions, need further guidance or simply want to share your progress, reach out to us on LinkedIn or social media. Let's keep the conversation going and build a community of creators and innovators.

Thank you for letting us be part of your journey. We look forward to seeing all the incredible and creative ideas you bring to life, making the world a more engaging, authentic place.

Here's to your success!
Alisha & Hamza

AUTHORS' BIOGRAPHY

Hamza Ayub is a trailblazer in the marketing world, celebrated for his remarkable achievements and innovative strategies. Ranked among Forbes 30 Under 30 in Marketing, he is currently the Chief Marketing Officer at Convenience House and Subway Switzerland. He previously held the position of Chief Marketing Officer at Dunkin' Switzerland, where he drove record-breaking success and garnered multiple prestigious awards. His expertise has made him a sought-after keynote speaker in numerous countries and a judge at some of the world's most renowned marketing competitions.

AUTHORS BIOGRAPHY

Alishquiche (Alisha Zoe de Munk) is a multi-award-nominated influencer with over 550,000 followers, regularly amassing 145 million views per quarter. On YouTube alone, her content has been watched more than 159 million times. Known for her relatable content in BookTok and pop culture, she has collaborated with leading brands and built a loyal global audience. Alishquiche's innovative approach makes her a pioneer in digital storytelling and engagement.